LEARN TO PLAY
HARMONICA

LEARN TO PLAY
HARMONICA

ILLUSTRATED TECHNIQUES FOR BLUES, ROCK, COUNTRY AND JAZZ

SANDY WELTMAN

CHARTWELL
BOOKS, INC.

This edition published in 2012 by Chartwell Books, Inc.,
A division of Book Sales, Inc.
276 Fifth Avenue Suite 206
New York, NY 10001
USA

ISBN: 978-0-7858-2908-9
QTT.HARM

A Quintet Book
Copyright © 2012 Quintet Publishing Limited
All rights reserved.

This book was conceived, designed, and produced by
Quintet Publishing Limited
The Old Brewery
6 Blundell Street
London N7 9BH
United Kingdom

Senior Editor: Liz Jones
Designer: Dominic Scott
Illustrations: Jeanne Weltman and Bernard Chau
Art Director: Michael Charles
Editorial Director: Donna Gregory
Publisher: Mark Searle

Printed in China by Midas Printing International Ltd.

9 8 7 6 5 4 3 2 1

CONTENTS ♫

♪ SONG LIST

INTRODUCTION ♫

Hi folks. I'm guessing that one of the reasons you bought this book is because you'd like to become a good harmonica player. I'm also guessing that you'd rather be playing the harmonica than sifting slowly through this or any other instruction book. In fact, you might be wondering if you can just skip this introduction and all of the stuff about technique and get right into playing a song or something? Well, no you can't really... so read on.

This book is not an exhaustive compilation of anything and everything to do with the harmonica, beginning with the first documented harmonica note to be blown by an unknown Kurdish shepherd in the year 1272 (made that one up!). However, this book will cover all the important elements needed to get you up and blowin' along with a lot of fun songs and blues licks as quickly as possible. It'll also cover some of the potential problems that have led many promising harmonica players astray.

Sound good? You might be interested in playing the blues with some buddies of yours in a small coffee shop down the street. This book can get you there. Maybe you want to impress all your co-workers (who thought you had absolutely no musical talent) at the next company picnic. This book can get you there. It's even possible that you have a dream to be the lead harmonica player in a punk rock band. This book (along with a new haircut) can get you there.

It all sounds great, right? However, you have a part in this too. You're probably thinking, uh oh, here comes the P word: practice, practice, practice. (Actually that's three words.) But what if I told you that with just a few minutes of practice a day, you could be jamming along on a few blues licks by the week's end? What if I told you that with just a few minutes of practice a day you could be playing in a blues band within the next six months? What if I told you that with just a few minutes invested each day, you could eventually become a rock legend and be chased into submission by the paparazzi?

You see, the possibilities are endless, but as I said above, you have a part in this. With just a few minutes a day, you can pursue some fun, a little passion, and a loving relationship. That might sound like your first crush, but I'm actually talking about the harmonica here.

People rarely succeed at what they endeavor to do unless they are having fun doing it. So, the most important thing to remember (next to breathing in and out while you play) is to have fun, and lots of it. Enjoy...

Sandy Weltman
www.sandyweltmanmusic.com

"People rarely succeed at what they endeavor to do unless they are having fun doing it. So, the most important thing to remember (next to breathing in and out while you play) is to have fun, and lots of it."

𝄞 HOW TO USE THIS BOOK

This is your book and as such you are free to skip around to any of the chapters in any order you like... Or, you can work through in the specific order in which it is laid out. Choose whichever way suits you best and keeps you engaged. However, it's best not to skip ahead of the first chapter before you have covered it thoroughly. This chapter will ground you in the basics that all the other chapters build on.

Each chapter includes songs and licks for you to enjoy working on. In fact, the only thing that might prevent you from enjoying them is by becoming frustrated when you can't hear any sound coming out of the harmonica as you play into it. That just might be because you're holding the harmonica backward, or it just might be because you skipped Chapter 1, Basic Techniques (!).

One way to teach harmonica is to use stories to get points across, or to explain a difficult concept. The stories in this book (labeled as "Story"!) are intended to encourage and enlighten you.

Take your harmonica and look closely inside this tiny four-inch piece of metal and wood. You'll find worlds of music inside of it. Anything that has worlds of anything inside it is bound to contain a few complicated or technical issues that it probably wouldn't hurt to address. (These will be marked as—get ready—"Technical".)

♪ CHAPTER 1: BASIC TECHNIQUES

2. Lip pursing (also affectionately known as pucker power). Lip pursing is all about forming your lips correctly over the harmonica. It's very similar to whistling—in fact, let's try that. Go ahead and whistle your favorite tune. As you do, look in the mirror and notice the shape of your lips. Now place the harmonica all the way in your mouth continuing to use the embouchure described earlier. The tiny little hole in your mouth that you saw in the mirror while you were whistling should now be directly in front of a hole with your top and bottom lips well over the cover plates. Try to keep the inside pucker tight with the outer lips relaxed. If you're still hearing a few notes played together, try to move the harmonica very slightly to the left or right so that it's centered over the hole.

3. The harmonica tilt. When all else fails, this is a sure thing. As you place the harmonica into your mouth, hold it so that the front side (with the holes) is tilted slightly down toward and into your lower lip (approximately a 45 degree angle). Conversely, the back end should be tilted up. The holes should be seated on the inside most part of your lower lip.

By tilting it this way, your lower lip partially blocks out the holes on each side of the hole you are trying to play. The tilt method is generally a good way to produce clean single notes. It can take a while until it becomes a permanent habit. Try to consciously tilt every time you put the harmonica in your mouth to play.

If you are still hearing more than one note, there is a good chance that your embouchure is too wide. If you've got a wide smile as you're trying for a single note, think tight pucker instead (more of a vertical opening). As you do this, make sure that the harmonica is still placed all of the way back in your mouth.

There are other approaches for achieving single notes. One of them is called tongue blocking, which sounds great for playing the blues, however it's a bit more difficult at first. Tongue blocking is covered in the last chapter (see page 176) but in the meantime work on lip pursing, it has its own advantages. Use the songs and exercises in the next chapter to help you develop your single notes.

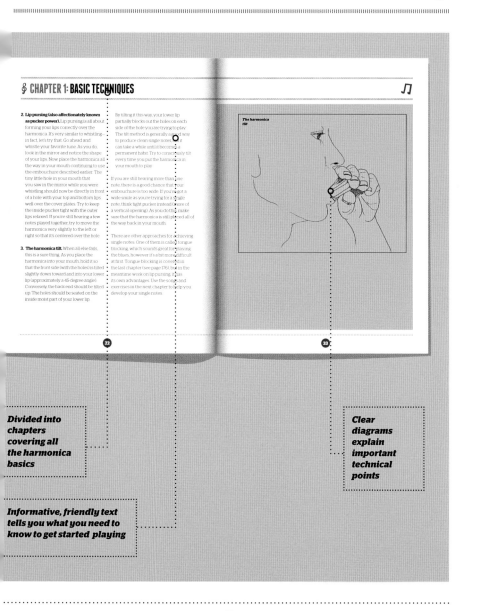

The harmonica tilt

Divided into chapters covering all the harmonica basics

Clear diagrams explain important technical points

Informative, friendly text tells you what you need to know to get started playing

𝄞 HOW TO USE THIS BOOK

The CD included with this book is designed to go hand in hand with all of the exercises and songs. Any time you see "***track #***," it means that there is a track of me demonstrating a particular lick, song, or exercise for you to listen to. Whenever you see "***rhythm track #***," that's a track for you to play along with. Consider the CD included with this book as your close friend, or at the very least your ex-boss's Uncle Fillmore that you met once at a company barbecue and who seemed kinda nice. Seriously though, the more you use the book and the CD together, the sooner you'll become a rock star (maybe!)... So do it often.

All of the tracks on the CD use a harmonica tuned to the key of C. The harmonica included with this book is also tuned to the key of C and should work fine to get you up and running. Once you're able to play some of the songs and exercises more comfortably, you might wish to upgrade. A better harmonica will naturally help you to play better. When you are ready to move up to a different model, check out the recommended harmonicas on page 194.

That about covers it, so unless you have any questions... let the games begin!

♪ CHAPTER 6: LICKS, LICKS, AND MORE LICKS

Five-beat triplet licks

This last set of triplet licks builds on the previous one by adding another group of triplets into the mix. These are played over a full measure (four beats) plus one beat in the next measure.

#6-24 2 3 4 – 4 5 4 – 4 3 2 – 2 ᶦ 2 – 2

#6-25 6 5 4 – 5 4 4 – 4 4 3 – 4 4 3 – 2

#6-26 4 5 4 4 3 4 4 4 3 4 4 3 2

#6-27 5 4 5 6 5 4 4 4 3 4 3 2 2

#6-28 3 4 5 5 5 4 3 4 5 4 4 3 2

Turnaround licks

Turnarounds happen on the last two measures of the 12-bar blues. The turnaround helps our ears to feel a resolution from the verse we've just played and then prepares our ears to hear a new verse. As such, turnarounds are a very important component of the blues. Here are three licks that work well over a turnaround.

#6-29 4 4 4 3 2 2 2 – 1 1

#6-30 2 2 3 3 4 4 4 2 – 1 1

#6-31 6 6 5 4 4 4 4 3 2 – 1 1

Tablature is used throughout to make learning melodies easy

Exercises are linked to the audio CD throughout for ease of understanding

♪ CHAPTER 1 ♫

BASIC
TECHNIQUES

♪ CHAPTER 1: BASIC TECHNIQUES

Before we start, let's introduce two close friends: Mr. Harmoni-can and Mr. Harmoni-can't. They each love to play the harmonica. They're both perfectly likeable, but their personalities are quite different.

Mr. Harmoni-can is a very intentional kind of guy. When he practices music, he always goes slowly and makes sure that he's following directions correctly. He's very patient. Someday he's going to be able to quit his day job and support his wife and 12 kids by playing the harmonica.

On the other hand, Mr. Harmoni-can't has very little patience. He always wants to be able to play everything right away and therefore rushes through most of his practice time. He's never taken the time to learn any proper techniques, such as holding the harmonica correctly or breathing into the harmonica the proper way. He'll never be a very good harmonica player (although he's a fabulous chess player).

"I finally realized why the harmonica is the world's most popular instrument—there's a 'sucker' born every minute."

♪ CHAPTER 1: BASIC TECHNIQUES

HOLDING THE HARMONICA (NOW THAT'S BASIC)

First, take the harmonica out of the case (there actually is no single correct way to do this, so be creative). Place the harmonica into your left hand with the holes facing you. Make sure that you can see the ten small numbers associated with each hole on top. If these ten numbers are not on top, you'll be holding the harmonica upside down and you'll have no choice but to play it standing on your head. This is a very difficult thing to do, so make sure you can see the ten numbers on top.

▶ Left hand

Place the thumb on your left hand lengthwise across the bottom of the harmonica and your index finger across the top. Bring the rest of the fingers in your left hand down so that they are parallel to your index finger. It's important that your left hand be set toward the back of the harmonica. If you're doing this correctly, you should be able to see approximately one-half to two-thirds of the top of the harmonica.

Does it feel as though the harmonica is going to slip easily from this highly touted left-hand grip, and tumble to the floor, shattering into 38 different pieces—effectively ending your harmonica career before it's even begun? If so, have no fear—the right hand is here.

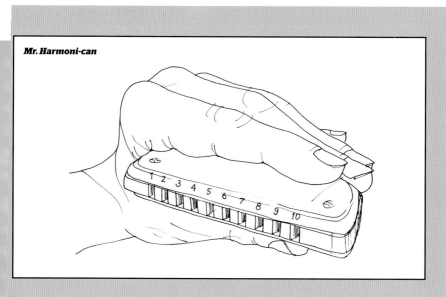

Mr. Harmoni-can

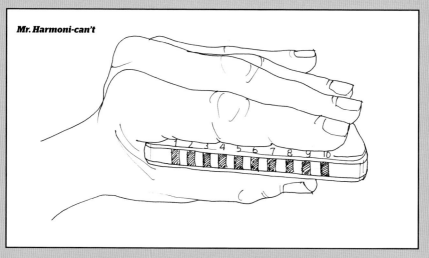

Mr. Harmoni-can't

♪ CHAPTER 1: BASIC TECHNIQUES

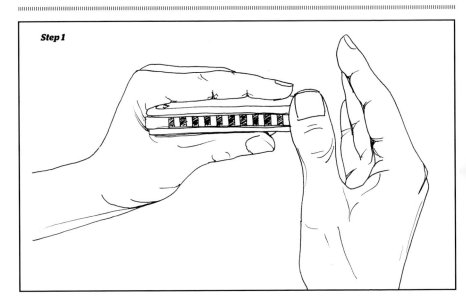

Step 1

▶ Right hand

The right hand is used for two reasons:
- ▶ To help support the harmonica.
- ▶ To help create an awesome little effect called **tremolo** (see page 163).

Step 1 Take the thumb on your right hand and place it on the front right corner (nearer the holes) of the harmonica so that it can pivot left and right.

Step 2 Pivot your right hand to the left so that it covers the back of your left hand.

Step 3 Now bring the heels of your palms together. Most of the harmonica, except for the holes and a bit of the front, should

be encased in your two hands. Feel free to experiment with moving the thumb on your right hand a bit, either to the left (covering a bit of holes nine and ten) or to the right side of the harmonica, or even underneath the harmonica. Everyone's hands are a different size, so experiment and see what feels best. You are now ready to play something...

Step 4 Put the harmonica to your lips and just blow out and breathe in (or "draw in") to get a feel for the instrument. Experiment for a few minutes playing on the different areas of the harmonica, but don't play it too hard.

Step 2

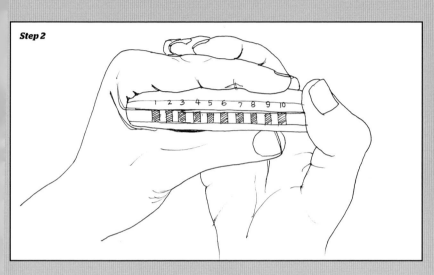

Step 3

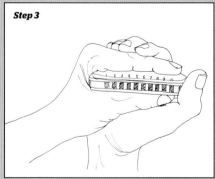

Mr. Harmoni-can't

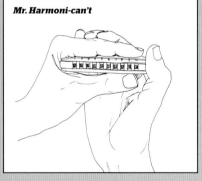

Wrong way/palms not together

𝄞 CHAPTER 1: BASIC TECHNIQUES

EMBOUCHURE (MORE THAN JUST A FANCY FRENCH WORD)

The French word *embouchure* has two different meanings. The first refers to the mouth of a river, and the second meaning is the adjustment of a player's mouth to the mouthpiece on his or her instrument. For our purposes, we'll be using the latter meaning, unless of course you're planning to take your harmonica on a canoe trip, in which case both meanings work well.

When it comes to the proper placement of the harmonica in the mouth, the ultimate goal is to ensure an airtight seal around each hole, or holes, with the mouth. If you can achieve this, the frustration factor will be significantly reduced. The proper way to do this is by getting the harmonica as deep into your mouth as possible (within reason, of course).

Bring the harmonica to your mouth. Try to place your lips over the middle part of the harmonica so that your upper lip is at least one-half (or more) the way over over the top of the harmonica and your bottom lip is about one-third of the way under the bottom of the harmonica. You'll want to place the instrument far enough into your mouth so that you can feel it touching the corners of your mouth where the top and bottom lips meet. You will eventually be moving the harmonica from hole to hole. When you do this, you'll want to slide it over the moist inner part of your lips.

Again, make sure that your left hand is far enough back from the holes. If it isn't, there's a good chance that you'll end up tasting your fingers. This is such a common beginner's mistake that you might think of it as the "Colonel Sanders position"... because it's finger-lickin' good (ouch!). For the first week or two you might find that your hands and lips are in a battle for position. Your job is to ensure a decisive lip victory.

If it all feels pretty strange, hang in there, it will get better shortly.

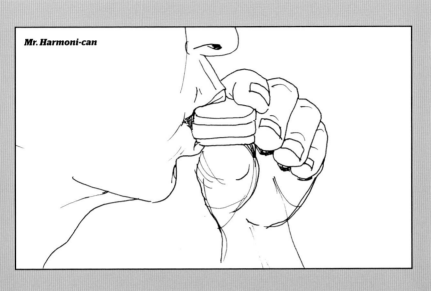

Mr. Harmoni-can

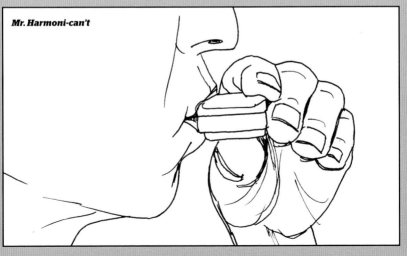

Mr. Harmoni-can't

BREATHING

At this point you might be hoping that you can skip over this section, as you most likely can already breathe. Be that as it may, you really should read on.

Breathing out is called "blowing" and breathing in is called "drawing"—and no, it's not called sucking even though you might hear that phrase being tossed recklessly about. I will say however, that if you learn to blow and draw correctly on the harmonica, then you will never suck (hope that one gets past my editor).

Proper breathing profoundly affects the three Ts—tone, technique, and timing—so you might as well get it right from the start.

Dos and don'ts of breathing
▸ *Don't play too hard on the harmonica. Most of the volume and intensity required to turn you into a screaming bluesman or blueswoman can be achieved by breathing gently and with good technique.*

▸ *Do play relaxed—and this means with your whole body. As the facial muscles, neck muscles, and so on become relaxed, so will your breathing. As the breathing is relaxed your throat will open up, helping you to produce a warm, lush tone. Everything is connected, so stay relaxed.*

TRY THIS

Take a big yawn as you breathe in. As you yawn, notice how your throat is open. That's what you're looking for as you gently breathe in and out of the harmonica.

STORY

Think finesse, not force

t's your birthday party and you're about to enjoy a double-fudge chocolate layer cake adorned with candles. As soon as the birthday song has finished you take in the biggest breath of your life and blow as hard as humanly possible while puffing your cheeks out... then silence—you did it. All of the candles appear to be extinguished. While this method can't be beat for blowing out candles on birthday cakes, it's also an example of the incorrect way to breathe while playing the harmonica... don't do that anymore.

Now imagine this...

Your cheeks are superglued in such a way that they are not able to expand or contract. With your mouth open, you begin to breathe in, whispering the word "ha." As you do so, your diaphragm begins to expand. Now you exhale with the word "huh," and your diaphragm contracts. You continue to do this, all the while imagining your breath traveling up and down a long wind tunnel from the bottom of your stomach, up past your lips, and out of your mouth. No ambulance is needed. This would be the correct way. Think finesse, not force.

So, just what is the nose supposed to be doing at this point? Absolutely nothing. Consider him on a break. We don't know when he'll be back, so keep him closed off for now. Later on, as you learn how to regulate your air better, the nose will return to the picture, and he'll help us to release a bit of that built-up air pressure or draw in some extra air as needed. Don't be too concerned with this for now though, because it will most likely happen naturally later on. The nose knows.

As for now, when you find yourself panting, puffing, and running out of air (a very common occurrence for beginners), try to remember to play gently using as little air as possible. One good method to more quickly learn how to regulate your air involves playing fiddle tunes. Many of these melodies employ a succession of fast notes (called eighth notes) played one right after another. Fiddle tunes are loads of fun to play and also a great way to learn breath control. You can find one of these tunes in Chapter 2 (see page 53).

> *"As for now, when you find yourself panting, puffing, and running out of air (a very common occurrence for beginners), try to remember to play gently using as little air as possible."*

♪ CHAPTER 1: BASIC TECHNIQUES

COMPING GROOVES (BREATHING PATTERNS)

These next few grooves will help with your breath control. You can use them to warm up with and they also sound great. For both of these patterns, you'll be covering your mouth over holes one, two, and three. Remember to use the correct embouchure. Listen to **track #1-1** first to hear what they sound like.

Now listen to me breathe Groove #1, which is the first half of the above patern. I'll breathe it three times through on **track #1-2**. Next, practice breathing it on your own until you're comfortable with it.

Groove #1

In (short pause) In In Out In In Out

Now let's add some articulations into the mix. We'll practice all of the articulations first and then add them to the breathing pattern.

Say the word "da" out loud. As you do, your tongue should be touching the roof of your mouth. Next breathe in as you whisper "da." Now for the "ka" sound. Practice "ka" the same way as you did with "da," saying it out loud first then breathing in as you whisper it. The last one is a "chu" sound. Say it out loud. Try making a crisp "ch" sound, like a snare drum. Practice this one on an out. You won't actually be blowing out, but rather just expelling air as you whisper the "chu." On the rest of the notes, make a "ha" sound as you breathe in and a "huh" sound as you breathe out.

Listen to the breathing of the pattern along with the articulations (without the harmonica) on **track #1-3**. You'll be able to really hear the air as I blow out on the "chu." Try to breathe along with the track.

In (pause) *In* *In* *Out* *In* *In* *Out*

Ha (pause) *Da* *Da* *Chu* *Ka* *Da* *Huh*

Now let's add the harmonica into the mix. Cover your mouth fully over holes one, two, and three and slowly try the pattern along with **track #1-4**.

Groove #2

Practice the breathing along with the track (without the harmonica) on **track #1-5**.

In *Out* *In* *In* *Out* *In* *In* *Out*

Ha *Huh* *Ha* *Da* *Chu* *Ka* *Da* *Huh*

Now listen to it with the harmonica and play along on **track #1-6**.

When you feel ready, put the two grooves together. Play along slowly with **track #1-7**.

♪ CHAPTER 1: BASIC TECHNIQUES

LEARNING TO PLAY SINGLE NOTES (ONE NOTE AT A TIME)

Having fun so far? Now it's time to learn to play one note at a time—affectionately known as single notes. Here's where we separate the men from the boys, the sheep from the goats... the Mr. Harmoni-cans from the Mr. Harmoni-can'ts.

As you've experimented up to this point, you've most likely been playing two and three notes at a time. These notes sound good when played together because they automatically harmonize with each other. However, much of the music you are going to want to learn to play involves sounding only one note at a time and that can be a bit more challenging than it sounds. First let's hear what a clean single note should sound like when blowing out on hole four. Listen to it on *track #1-8*.

Can you hear the difference?

Let's try playing a single note. Using the same embouchure as described earlier, place your mouth/lips over hole one. Try to produce a single note by blowing gently.

Did you do it? If so, that's good news. However, the bad news is that it generally gets a bit harder to produce single notes as you move past hole one, but don't despair (at least not yet).

Now let's try the same thing on hole four. Place the harmonica in your mouth, again making sure to use the correct embouchure. Try to center your mouth over hole four and blow gently. Did you get a single note? If not, now you can despair... but only for a few seconds, because here are a few how-to tips that will help you achieve clean single notes.

1. **The most important thing: embouchure.** Do not, I repeat DO NOT, sacrifice your embouchure for the sake of getting a single note. While it is easier at first to achieve a single note with the harmonica being not so deep in your mouth, you will lose a lot of other things in the process, like good tone, note bending, playing cleanly, etc. Is all that really worth it? Probably not.

Quick note of encouragement

Working on all of these techniques can certainly be frustrating at times, but be patient and hang in there with it. If you can work on your technique for just a few minutes each day, within a few short weeks you'll start observing noticeable improvements in your playing.

Many times you'll work on something for a while and feel as though you aren't making an ounce of progress. Then, when you're least expecting it, you'll pick up the harmonica and voilà, all of a sudden you've got it down. Progress often happens this way.

If all else fails, put the harmonica down for a few days and come back to it. If nothing else, when you return to play you'll find your frustration factor has significantly reduced.

The great harmonica paradox, and also the moral of all of this is:

When it comes to making progress and it feels like nothing is happening, something usually is.

2. Lip pursing (also affectionately known as pucker power). Lip pursing is all about forming your lips correctly over the harmonica. It's very similar to whistling—in fact, let's try that. Go ahead and whistle your favorite tune. As you do, look in the mirror and notice the shape of your lips. Now place the harmonica all the way in your mouth continuing to use the embouchure described earlier. The tiny little hole in your mouth that you saw in the mirror while you were whistling should now be directly in front of a hole with your top and bottom lips well over the cover plates. Try to keep the inside pucker tight with the outer lips relaxed. If you're still hearing a few notes played together, try to move the harmonica very slightly to the left or right so that it's centered over the hole.

3. The harmonica tilt. When all else fails, this is a sure thing. As you place the harmonica into your mouth, hold it so that the front side (with the holes) is tilted slightly down toward and into your lower lip (approximately a 45-degree angle). Conversely, the back end should be tilted up. The holes should be seated on the inside moist part of your lower lip.

By tilting it this way, your lower lip partially blocks out the holes on each side of the hole you are trying to play. The tilt method is generally a good way to produce clean single notes, but it can take a while until it becomes a permanent habit. Try to consciously tilt every time you put the harmonica in your mouth to play.

If you are still hearing more than one note, there is a good chance that your embouchure is too wide. If you've got a wide smile as you're trying for a single note, think tight pucker instead (more of a vertical opening). As you do this, make sure that the harmonica is still placed all of the way back in your mouth.

There are other approaches for achieving single notes. One of them is called tongue blocking, which sounds great for playing the blues, however it's a bit more difficult at first. Tongue blocking is covered in the last chapter (see page 176), but in the meantime work on lip pursing; it has its own advantages. Use the songs and exercises in the next chapter to help you develop your single notes.

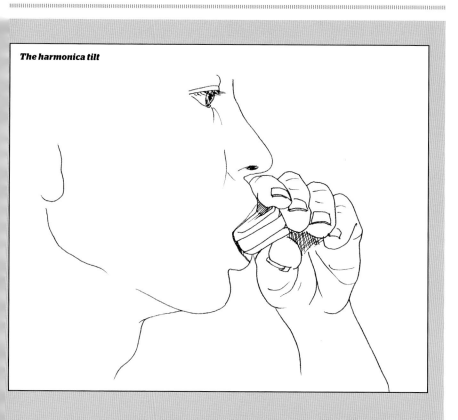

The harmonica tilt

𝄞 CHAPTER 1: BASIC TECHNIQUES

READING HARMONICA MUSIC (TABLATURE)

Before getting stuck into the songs and exercises, here's a 60-second lesson on reading harmonica music.

Harmonica tablature is sooooo easy to read. You don't have to know how to read standard music notation to begin reading harmonica music.

The number denotes which hole on the harmonica to play into. A vertical line above the number denotes blowing out (a blow note):

Example: 4̍ means to blow out on hole four. A vertical line below the number denotes breathing in (a draw note):

Example: 5̣ means to breathe in on hole five.

Sometimes you'll see the numbers grouped closer together. This means to play all of those notes simultaneously.

The following is an example:

4̍ 4̣ 5̍ 4̣ 3̍4̍5̍

Hole four is blown out and then drawn in. Next hole five is blown out followed by the draw on hole four. Finally holes three, four, and five are all blown at the same time. Later on, as we get into bending notes (Chapter 6), we'll add a few more notation signs.

It's important to listen to the audio examples on the CD. This will allow you to correctly hear all of the rhythms and assorted nuances.

CHAPTER 2 ♫

SCALES, MELODIES, TRAIN SOUNDS

THIS SECTION:

PLAYING THE MAJOR SCALE

Now that you've learned a few tips about getting single notes, it's time to put them into practice. The goal of these next few exercises is to not only solidify your embouchure and single notes, but to train your ears as well.

The major scale contains seven notes that all tend to gravitate toward what you might call the "home base note." For instance, if you play a C major scale, your ear usually wants to resolve back to a C, which would be your home base note. You'll recognize the major scale as *do-re-mi-fa-so-la-ti-do*. Thousands of melodies and simple folk songs use only the notes found in the major scale. By learning and assimilating the major scale into your playing, you'll be able to pick out many of those songs on your own, without the use of any music notation.

You'll be playing everything in this chapter in first position. First position just means that you are playing a song in the same key the harmonica is tuned to (much more on this to follow!). A letter denoting the key the harmonica is tuned to is usually stamped in one of the corners on the top cover plate (the metal part of the harmonica).

The first position major scale is found at three different places on the harmonica. The first octave is holes one through four, the second octave is on holes four through seven, and the third octave is on holes seven through ten. First listen to what it sounds like in the second octave played with single notes (***track # 2-1***).

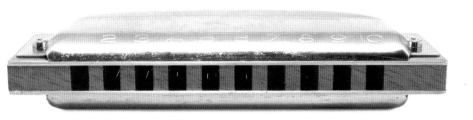

♪ CHAPTER 2: SCALES, MELODIES, TRAIN SOUNDS

You'll be playing the major scale, and also the next few exercises and songs, in the middle octave or middle part of the harmonica (holes four to seven). This is where all of the notes in the first position major scale can be fully accessed without having to "bend" notes (discussed later on in Chapter 7). Before you try the major scale on your own, here are four important tips worth mentioning:

▶ Never take the harmonica away from your lips as you switch from hole to hole.

▶ When switching from one hole to another hole, slide the harmonica along the inside, moist part of your lips. Use your lower lip as a guide.

▶ You might find yourself losing the single note when you slide to a new hole. Most people are a bit tentative when sliding to an adjacent hole. If this happens, go ahead and slide over just a bit farther than you think you need to. Make sure to center your mouth over the hole.

▶ Go slowly at first. After you can play it cleanly, then try gradually speeding it up.

After a while, all of this will start to feel very natural. Go ahead and give it a try very slowly on your own.

Before you practice, it's a good idea to listen to the CD as you try to imitate the sound. How you practice is how you're going to play, and how you play is how you're going to sound. If you practice choppy, you're going to end up playing and sounding choppy. If you practice with big round connected notes, you're going to sound awesome, so listen often, slow it down, and get it sounding good.

Major scale

SCALE NOTES: C D E F G A B C

HARMONICA TAB:

4 4 5 5 6 6 7 7

The scale is slowed down on *track # 2-2*. When you feel ready, try playing along.

Now try playing the scale starting on hole seven blow and going down. Try practicing slowly going up and down with *track # 2-3*.

As you practice these exercises and songs, try to make the notes sound big and full. Make sure they're not choppy but connect smoothly to each other.

PATTERNS AND ARPEGGIOS

Another great way to work with scales is by practicing them in patterns. A pattern is just a different way of rearranging the notes.

Leapfrog up

This next exercise is called a leapfrog pattern. Even though it still contains all the notes of the C major scale, it's going to sound very different because the notes are now sequenced differently (in a different order) from the first exercise. Give it a listen on *track # 2-4*, then try playing it slowly on your own. Remember, your main goal here is to be able to play clear, clean single notes.

Leapfrog down

Now try playing it going down. Listen on *track # 2-5*.

Up three and back

This fun pattern starts on the first note in the scale. It goes up three notes then back to the first note. Next it starts on the second note in the scale going up three and back to that second note in the scale. Then it starts on the third note in the scale, and so on. It's a very musical pattern and very fun to play. Make sure to listen first on *track # 2-6*.

Descending

When you feel ready, try playing it slowly up and down with *track # 2-7*.

See over the page for the exercises.

#2-4 Leapfrog up

C E D F E G F A G B A C B D C

4 5 4 5 5 6 5 6 6 7 6 7 7 8 7

#2-5 Leapfrog down

7 6 7 6 6 5 6 5 5 4 5 4 4 3 4

#2-6 Up three and back

4 4 5 4 - 4 5 5 4 - 5 5 6 5 - 5 6 6 5 - 6 6 7 6

6 7 7 6 - 7 7 8 7 - 7

#2-7 Descending

7 7 6 7 - 7 6 6 7 - 6 6 5 6 - 6 5 5 6 —

5 5 4 5 — 5 4 4 5 - 4 4 3 4 - 4

Arpeggio exercises

An arpeggio is a chord that is played one note at a time instead of the notes being played simultaneously (for more on chords, see page 99). Arpeggios can be great fun to practice.

Ascending

This exercise will really help to open your ears (**track # 2-8**).

Descending

Here's a similar exercise, except now you'll be starting on hole eight blow and going down (**track # 2-9**).

See over the page for the exercises.

Definition
An arpeggio is a chord that is played one note at a time instead of the notes being played simultaneously.

#2-8 **Ascending**

4 5 6   4 5 6   5 6 7   5 6 7   6 7 8   6 7 8

7 8 9 7

#2-9 **Descending**

8 7 6   8 7 6   7 6 5   7 6 5   6 5 4   6 5 4

5 4 3 4

SIMPLE MELODIES

*G. Love performs in
Munich, Germany*

Now you're going to play some songs.
Listen to each one first, then try playing it
on your own or with the CD. Remember,
one of your goals here is to be able to
produce clean, clear single notes.

🎼 CHAPTER 2: SCALES, MELODIES, TRAIN SOUNDS

#2-10 Oh Shenandoah

3 4 4 4 4 5 6 6 6 7 7 6 6 6 6 5 6

6 6 6 5 6 5 4 4 3 4 3 4 6 6

3 4 4 5 4 4 4

#2-11 When the Saints Go Marching In

4 5 5 6 4 5 5 6 4 5 5 6 5 4 5 4

5 4 4 4 5 6 6 6 5 5 5 6 5 4 4

#2-12 You Are My Sunshine

3 4 4 5 5 5 4 5 4 4 4 4 5 5 6 6 6 5 5

4 4 5 5 6 6 6 5 5 4 4 4 5 5 4 4 5 4

48

#2-13 Beethoven's Ninth

5 5 5 6 6 5 5 4 4 4 4 5 5 4 4

5 5 5 6 6 5 5 4 4 4 4 5 4 4 4

4 5 4 4 5 5 5 4 4 5 5 5 4 4 4 3

5 5 5 6 6 5 5 4 4 4 4 5 4 4 4

#2·14 **Oh Susannah**

4 4 5 6 6 6 6 5 4 4 5 5 4 4 4

4 4 5 6 6 6 6 5 4 4 5 5 4 4 4

5 5 6 6   6 6 5 4 4

4 4 5 6 6 6 6 5 4 4 5 5 4 4 4

Minuet in G

Here is a familiar tune, written in the seventeenth century, that was originally credited to Johann Sebastian Bach. The same melody was used for the 1965 pop hit "A Lovers' Concerto."

Great song, great melody. We're going to be playing it on a C harmonica in the key of C. See over the page.

"You might find that the draw notes feel a bit stuck or make no sound at all. If this is the case, try to draw with less of a 'sucking in' motion at the front of your mouth. Try breathing from deeper down in your diaphragm."

#2-15 **Minuet in G: A section (played once)**

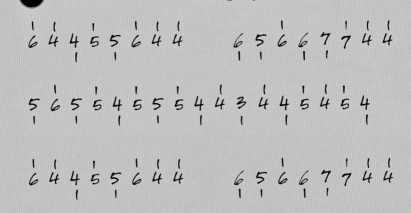

```
6 4 4 5 5 6 4 4    6 5 6 6 7 7 4 4

5 6 5 5 4 5 5 5 4 4 3 4 4 5 4 5 4

6 4 4 5 5 6 4 4    6 5 6 6 7 7 4 4

5 6 5 5 4 5 5 5 4 4 4 5 4 4 3 4
```

Blackberry Blossom (fiddle tune)

Here's a nifty little fiddle tune (**track # 2-16**), which will help you learn to regulate your breathing so that you are able to conserve more air. As you become more proficient at playing the song, try to gradually increase the tempo. As you do this, begin to back off slightly with your breathing. Each section is played two times.

"As you become more proficient at playing the song, try to gradually increase the tempo."

#2-16 **A section (played two times)**

7 8 8 7 7 7 8 7 6 7 7 6 6 5 5

5 6 6 5 5 6 5 5 6 6 5 5 4

7 8 8 7 7 7 8 7 6 7 7 6 6 5 5

5 6 6 5 5 6 5 5 4 4 3 4 4   2x thru

#2-16 **B section (played two times)**

5 – 6 5 6 6 – 5 6 6 5 6 5 4 4

5 – 6 5 6 – 6 7 7 7 7 8 7 7 6 6

5 – 6 5 6 6 – 5 6 6 5 6 5 4 4

7 7 7 6 6 7 6 5 5 4 4 3 4   2x thru

FABULOUS TRAIN SOUNDS

All good harmonica players learn to play a few good train sounds. It's a prerequisite for entertaining your five-year-old daughter and her friends for an hour-and-a-half while your wife is getting her hair done. Your dog will love it as well.

Method 1

There are lots of different ways to make train sounds on the harmonica. We'll start with a pretty basic one. Both of these train sounds involve playing more than one note at a time.

Cover your mouth over holes one, two, and three, making sure you are using the correct embouchure. Next, breathe in twice and then breathe out twice, slowly continuing this pattern. Add a "da" (tongue articulation from Chapter 1, see page 28) to the second group of notes. That's pretty much it. Listen to it on **track # 2-17**, then try it slowly on your own.

Some of the notes may feel a bit stuck. If this happens, try keeping your mouth relaxed and open on the inside while also keeping your nose open. Practice it slowly at first, but for full effect, you'll eventually want to pick up the tempo. For a variation on this, do the train sound as above, but on the second time through draw in only on hole one (**track # 2-18**).

For another variation, make the last group of notes a draw instead of a blow. Add a "da" to the first and second group of notes (**track # 2-19**).

Now try combining the two variations, as on the next page (**track # 2-20**).

𝄞 CHAPTER 2: SCALES, MELODIES, TRAIN SOUNDS

#2-17

```
     ' | |   ' | |                      ' | |   ' | |
123  123  123  123        123  123  123  123  etc...
' ' '  ' ' '               ' ' '  ' ' '
     da                        da
```

#2-18

```
     ' | |   ' | |                      ' | |   ' | |
123  123  123  123        '    '    123  123  etc...
' ' '  ' ' '              '    '
     da                   da
```

#2-19

```
     ' | |
123  123  123  123
' ' '  ' ' '       ' ' '
da   da
```

#2-20

123   123   123   123   123   123 etc...

      da   da

123   123   123   123   123   123 etc...

      da   da

or

123   123   123   123   123   123   123   123

da   da   da   da

123   123   123   123   123   123 etc...

da   da   da

♪ CHAPTER 2: SCALES, MELODIES, TRAIN SOUNDS

Method 2

This next train sound is fun as well, but quite different from the previous one.

Say the word "chu." Now whisper it while emphasizing the "ch" part of it. Try it again, this time keeping your mouth opened up only slightly. Place your hand up a few inches in front of your mouth and try the "chu" sound one more time. Can you feel the air coming from your mouth when you do it? There is no need to actually blow out air. The air that is coming from your mouth as you do a "chu" is all the air that will be necessary to make this part of the train sound.

Now say "kuh." Next whisper it. Can you feel the "kuh" coming from your throat? Just as with the "chu" sound, a bit of air should be coming from your mouth when you are making the "kuh" sound. Again, as you practice these two sounds, make sure that you are not blowing air out but rather expelling it naturally during the sound.

Next put the two sounds together, "chu-kuh." You're almost there. Now breathe in trying to make a very soft "ah" sound from your throat. Finally, put it all together. Make the "ah" (in) sound first and then the "chu-kuh" (out) next. Listen to it on **track # 2-21**, then you try it.

Now try it with the harmonica. Cover your mouth over holes one, two, and three:

"ah-chu-kuh ah-chu-kuh ah-chu-kuh" etc...

Listen to **track # 2-22**. Now add on another "chu-kuh" so that it's:

"ah-chu-kuh chu-kuh ah-chu-kuh chu-kuh" etc. (**track # 2-23**).

Add yet another "chu-kuh" to the mix, making it:

"ah-chu-kuh chu-kuh chu-kuh ah-chu-kuh chu-kuh chu-kuh" etc. (**track # 2-24**).

Finally (really!), to make a full nice-sounding train, you'll want to add 76 more "chu-kuhs"... (Just kidding!) But after reading that, you'll be relieved to know that you'll only need four more for a total of seven "chu-kuhs." Try it out slowly. "ah-chu-kuh chu-kuh chu-kuh chu-kuh chu-kuh chuh-kuh chu-kuh"

As you gradually increase the tempo a very nice train sound will start to emerge.

CHAPTER 2: SCALES, MELODIES, TRAIN SOUNDS ♫

Track # 2-25 starts out slowly and gradually increases the tempo. Count the "chu-kuhs" as you listen (perhaps no one's ever said that to you before).

A variation on this train sound would be to replace the "chu-kuh" with a "too-kuh." Try it out and see which one you like best.

The train whistle

No matter how amazingly well you do a train sound on the harmonica, it will still feel incomplete without the fabulous train whistle at its side.

For the train whistle, you'll only be using holes three and four. Cover your mouth over these two holes and breathe in twice, going for a "wah-wah" sound. You can also try it with one long breath in, but trying to separate that breath into three parts. You do this bit by dropping your tongue down and back a bit while trying to form an "oh" sound. Listen on *track # 2-26*.

One long breath in "wah_____oh_____wah" tongue drops.

When you feel ready, try to combine different train sounds with the train whistle. As you start to be able to accomplish this, you will definitely be on the right track (completely unapologetic pun intended).

$\mathcal{G}$ CHAPTER 3 ♫
HARMONICA
POSITIONS

THIS SECTION:

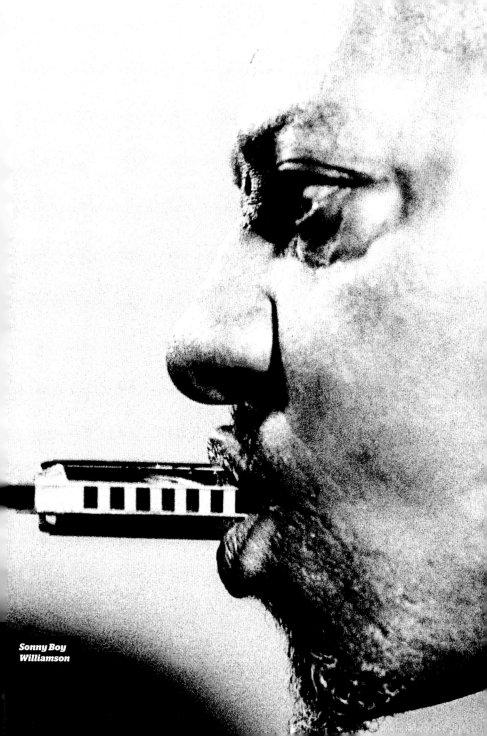

Sonny Boy Williamson

CHAPTER 3: HARMONICA POSITIONS

UNDERSTANDING HARMONICA POSITIONS

One of the most confusing and least understood elements of playing the harmonica is the concept of "harmonica positions." It's also one of the most important. But what exactly is a harmonica position? Before that can be answered, you first need to understand what a position is not.

The term "position" does not refer to a physical position, such as playing on the top or bottom end of the harmonica. It also has no relationship to practicing your harmonica in yoga class while attempting a lunge pose.

A harmonica position is the terminology used to help identify the relationship between the key a song is in and the key the harmonica is tuned to. The two are often different, and that's especially true for playing the blues. Understanding the principles of harmonica positions will allow you to choose which key harmonica will be best suited to whatever particular song you want to play. We're going to delve deeper into all of this, but first a short story...

STORY

Let's say that you're stranded on Gilligan's Island with only one harmonica in the key of C. There's no good reason to bring more than one—after all, it's only a three-hour tour. Unbeknown to anyone on board, the skipper had a very shady past, which included a six-year stint playing slide guitar in a rundown shanty on the bad side of Memphis. Never without an instrument at his side, the skipper took along his slide guitar, just in case a blues jam were to break out. After being stranded for more than a week and with boredom setting in, the skipper, as leader, realizes that he needs to liven things up. He pulls his beat-up old guitar out of his dusty case and begins grooving on a blues shuffle in the key of G.

Wanting to get in on the action, and especially to impress Ginger, you pull out your C harmonica and start jamming along with the skipper. Ginger smiles at you warmly. At this point there's no need to worry about harmonica positions because you have no choice in the matter concerning which key harmonica you should use to jam along with the skipper. You only brought one harmonica along with you. You're such a great player that you can easily jam along with the skipper in the key of G while playing on a C harmonica. Ginger melts into your arms.

Had this story been different and had you known ahead of time that you were going to be shipwrecked, you might not have gotten on board. At the very least you might have considered taking along your tackle box full of 12 harmonicas, one for each key. However, had that happened, you might have found yourself in a real quandary. Which key harmonica would you have used to play the blues along with the skipper in the key of G? On the surface, using a G harmonica seems obvious and straightforward, but you've experimented with that before and discovered that playing the blues in the same key as the harmonica is tuned in is about as soulful as Kate Smith singing "Up With People."

There're so many harmonicas and so many choices. What's a bluesman or blueswoman to do? You're about to miss out on making a striking impression with Ginger, although Mary Ann sure seems nice and she bakes well too... This is where understanding harmonica positions can really pay off, even if you never get shipwrecked.

This story was intended to lighten the mood—it can be frustrating when you don't fully understand everything there is to know about harmonica positions. If this is you, please don't be overly concerned. If you don't grasp all of this right away (and you won't), it will start to make more sense the more you play, so just keep playing.

With that said, and to get you playing along with friends as soon as possible, there's a position chart included at the end of this chapter. This chart will tell you which key harmonica you need to use for whatever key the song is in. If only you had bought this book before that cruise...

♪ CHAPTER 3: HARMONICA POSITIONS

TECHNICAL STUFF

Since harmonica positions have everything to do with key, let's first understand what a key is.

What is a key?

A key identifies the tonal center or home base of a song. This tonal center or home base is a specific note that the whole song generally revolves around. All of the notes in a song usually want to gravitate toward that specific home base note. For example, if a song is in the key of C, then every note in the song gravitates or resolves toward C (like the major scale we talked about earlier). If a song is in the key of G, then every note usually will tend to gravitate toward G.

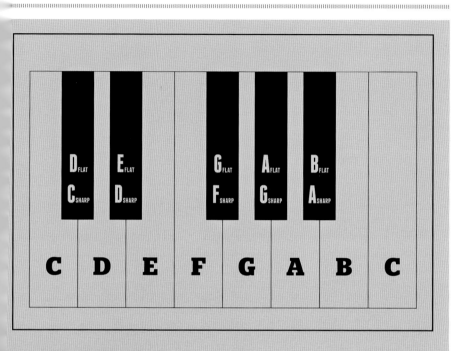

Looking at the piano diagram, we can better visualize the notes in relation to each other when thinking about key. Here, one octave on the piano keyboard is shown.

♪ CHAPTER 3: HARMONICA POSITIONS

MORE TECHNICAL STUFF

There are 12 notes (pitches) in music. They are:

A, A sharp, B, C, C sharp, D, D sharp,

E, F, F sharp, G, G sharp

Sharps and flats are the black keys on a piano. For example, C sharp is the next note up after C; G flat is the next note down after G. Sharps and flats are actually the same notes, but with different names (C sharp is also D flat). The 12 notes make up a range of one octave. C to C is an octave. A to A is an octave, and so on. The ten-hole diatonic harmonica has a range of three full octaves.

Each note has a key that is associated with it. Since there are 12 different notes in music, there are also 12 different keys. Each key contains a specific set of notes that belong exclusively to it. For example, the key of C contains these notes:

C, D, E, F, G, A, B, C

which is the same major scale we played in the previous chapter (see page 38).

The key of G has these notes associated with it:

G, A, B, C, D, E, F sharp, G

Notice that the key of C has an F in it and the key of G has an F sharp.

Listen to the C major scale first, followed by the G major scale on *track # 3-1*.

Both scales are major scales and sound like do-re-mi-fa-so-la-ti-do. The reason for that is because the relationship (distance) between one note and the next in each scale is the same. That means that if you play a song on a harmonica in the key of G and then play it the exact same way on a harmonica in the key of C, the same song will come out. It will just be in a different key. That works with any diatonic (ten-hole) harmonica in any key.

Since there are 12 different keys in music, there are also 12 different harmonica positions. That means that you have 144 choices of approach to playing any song... But before you close this book for good and place your harmonica back on the shelf forever, relax... You will never need to be able to play in all of those positions to become a great harmonica player. You just need to be aware of the endless possibilities of this powerful little instrument. The main thing to understand about all of this is that each position on a harmonica has its own very unique sound and feel.

The design and original intent for the harmonica, was to be played in only one position (or key), which we call first position. Remember, first position (also called "straight harp") means that you are playing in the key that the harmonica

is tuned to. Everything you played in Chapter 2 was in first position.

First position is great for playing certain melodies and songs, but not so great for playing the blues or for playing songs in a minor key (as opposed to major key). Over the next few chapters we'll be focusing on two new positions: second position and third position. Second position works great for playing blues on harmonica. More on that later, but for now, let's find out more about third position.

THIRD POSITION

Third position (also called slant harp) works well for playing in minor keys. It can be quite bluesy as well. At this point if you're unsure about minor vs. major, listen to **track # 3-2**. The major chord will sound first, followed by a minor chord.

To get a better feel for and to understand the differences between major and minor, think of them in terms of images. For instance, a major key might appear as happy, bright, and sunny while a minor key tends to be more sad, dark, and melancholy.

Third position means that you are playing a song one whole step higher than the key of the harmonica. For instance, **track # 3-3** is "Scarborough Fair" in the key of D minor on a C harmonica. If it were played on an A harmonica, it would be in the key of B minor, and so on...

Dorian scale

"Scarborough Fair" is a very old British folk song made popular Simon and Garfunkel. The melody is based on a type of minor scale called a dorian scale. Listen to the scale first on **track # 3-4**, then you try it out. As you practice it up and down, notice its melancholy flavor compared to the brighter sounding major scale.

Scarborough Fair

CONGRATULATIONS! You've just played a scale in third position. Now let's try out "Scarborough Fair." Listen again on **track # 3-3**.

> "A major key might appear as happy, bright, and sunny while a minor key tends to be more sad, dark, and melancholy."

#3-4 Dorian scale

d   e   f   g   a   b   c   d

4   5   5   6   6   7   7   8

#3-3 Scarborough Fair (third position)

4 4 6 6 5 5 5 4   6 7 8 7 6 7 6 6

8 8 8 7 6 6 6 5 5 4   4 6 6 5 5 4 4 4

73

SECOND POSITION

Second position (also called cross harp) is probably the most commonly used position today. It works with the blues, bluegrass, country, and jazz as well.

Each position has its own unique sound and feel. As you start out, first position is going to have more of an even balance of blow and draw notes, while second position focuses more on the draw notes.

Second position means that you are playing a song in a key that is a fourth up from the key of the harmonica. For instance, *track #5-6* is "Harmonica Boogie" in the key of G on a C harmonica. A fourth up, or four notes up the G major scale, leads us to C (G-A-B-C-D-E-F#-G). If you were playing a song in the key of A in second position, you would need to use a harmonica tuned to D—if you count four notes up the A scale, you come to D.

Positions help identify the relationship between **the key a song is in** and **the key of the harmonica it is being played on.**

Blues licks
Here are a few blues licks to give you a feel for second position (see opposite page). You can combine these licks in any order to make longer licks.

Listen first to *track #3-8*, then try experimenting by playing them in a different order.

Obviously, another important element of the blues is learning to play the correct bluesy notes and stay away from the "just a white boy singing the blues" kind of notes—and that leads us right up to the fake blues scale...

ARE YOU A BIT OUT OF BREATH?
If so, that's perfectly normal. Because second position tends to incorporate more draw notes than blow notes, you will most likely feel a little out of breath until you can learn to regulate your air flow more efficiently.

#3-5 Lick 1

```
                I I I                        I I I
123  123  234  123   -   123  123  234  123        etc...
I I I  I I I      I I I      I I I  I I I      I I I
```

#3-6 Lick 2

```
           I I I                              I I I
234  234  345  234  123  -  234  234  345  234  123  etc...
I I I  I I I      I I I I I I    I I I  I I I      I I I I I I
```

#3-7 Lick 3

```
                I I I  I I I                   I I I  I I I
123  123  234  123      123  123  234  123
I I I  I I I          I I I  I I I
```

```
                I I I  I I I
123  123  234  123  123
I I I  I I I          I I I
```

♪ CHAPTER 3: HARMONICA POSITIONS

THE FAKE BLUES SCALE (IN SECOND POSITION)

After reading the title above, you're probably asking "Why am I going to learn a 'fake' blues scale instead of the real thing?" The answer is that unfortunately we'd have to charge you more for the book if we were to show you the real one... Just kidding—actually, that's a great question. The real answer is that all of the notes required to play the "real" blues scale aren't technically on the harmonica.

Fortunately for us and all blues lovers around the globe, these notes can be accessed by employing a series of four techniques called draw bending, blow bending, over-blowing, and over-drawing. These are challenging techniques to learn at first, but well worth the effort, and this subject is discussed more in Chapter 7. In the meantime, the reason we use the "fake blues scale" is that it's very close to the real blues scale and all of the notes are there on the harmonica and can be easily accessed just by blowing and drawing as normal.

But you might then ask "Does this mean that all of the licks and songs I'll be learning with the fake blues scale won't be the real deal"? Absolutely not. Tons of great licks and songs can be played using only the notes in the fake blues scale, as you shall soon see—first give it a listen on *track # 3-9*.

The fake blues scale

G	B	C	D	F	G
2	3	4	4	5	6
↑	↑	↓	↑	↑	↑

Is that all there is to the fake blues scale? Yep, that's it. Pretty simple-looking but very profound, musically speaking. Go ahead and try playing it slowly on your own. Practice it forward and backward until you have it memorized. You'll be using it in the very next exercise.

The Blues
Brothers

♪ CHAPTER 3: HARMONICA POSITIONS

THE ONE-NOTE BLUES JAM

"Jamming" is just a much cooler way of saying improvising. On this next exercise that's exactly what we'll be learning to do, using the fake blues scale.

Most improvised music contains two important elements: melody and rhythm. The melody is comprised of the notes that we choose to play. Rhythm is the duration and timing of those notes as they relate to each other.

We want to start off our first jam session by limiting the amount of notes (melody) that we'll be using. This is so we can keep our creative side focused on just the rhythm, at least for now. As we move forward with this exercise, we'll be adding more notes from the fake blues scale one at a time. The first note we'll be working with is a D note found on the hole-four draw.

Let's start with a set rhythm that we can eventually expand on. First listen to the rhythm on **track # 3-10** using only the hole-four draw. Notice that this rhythm contains six beats or pulses. Play it along with the CD to help you remember it.

A little trick you can use to remember a rhythm is to assign a short sentence to it that has the same amount of syllables as there are beats in the rhythm. In this case the rhythm contains six beats, so practice it by speaking it along with a six-syllable sentence. Here are a few examples. Try speaking them using the same rhythm that's on **track # 3-10**.

"I'm eat-ing beans and rice," or "I'm gon-na be a star," or "I'll buy this book a-gain." Got the idea?

Next we'll add some variations to the rhythm. Listen to an example on **track # 3-11**.

Now you try it. Make up your own variations to complement the original rhythm and play along with rhythm **track # 3-12** using only the hole-four draw. Resist the urge to play any other notes. Do it over and over until you can feel the creative juices starting to flow.

Now let's add in the hole-four blow from the fake blues scale. Go through the same exercise as above but this time try improvising the rhythm using only these two notes, the hole-four draw, and the hole-four blow. Keep thinking rhythmically. Listen to an example on **track # 3-13**.

Next, we'll jam on three notes by adding the five-hole draw from the fake blues scale. Do the same thing as above and keep the creative rhythms coming. Every time we add a new note from the fake blues scale, jam along with the music

on **rhythm track # 3-12** until you feel comfortable with it.

Next add in the hole-six blow.

Now add in the hole-three draw.

Finally insert the hole-two draw. Listen to an example using all of the notes from the fake blues scale on **track # 3-14**.

Did you make it this far? You probably did since you're here. How did it feel? Go back to this exercise often, continually trying out new ideas.

One important word before we move on. That word is SPACE. As it's been stated, space is the final frontier, but it's also your musical friend. Leaving space between notes and phrases not only gives the listeners' ears a break, but also makes the notes that we do play sound even better. Use it often.

HARMONICA POSITIONS CHART

Here is a chart to help you work out which key harmonica to use with the key any particular song is in. Since we've covered the first three harmonica positions, those are what you will find in this chart.

As you look at the far left column, you will see the harmonica keys going down vertically. As you move to the right, you will see in each box the key of the song under the position columns. Let's say a song is in the key of E and you will be playing it in second position. To find out what key harmonica you would need to use, go down the second position column and find the E (song key). Next, move to the far left column under "Key of harmonica." You should come to an A, which is the key of the harmonica you need to use.

There are two scenarios that you will eventually need to consider with regard to harmonica positions (see over).

KEYS OF HARMONICA AND POSITIONS

Key of harmonica	First position key of song (straight harp)	Second position key of song (cross harp)	Third position key of song
G	G	D	Am
A flat	A flat	E flat	B flat m
A	A	E	Bm
B flat	B flat	F	Cm
B	B	F sharp	C sharp m
C	C	G	Dm
D flat	D flat	A flat	E flat m
D	D	A	Em
E flat	E flat	B flat	Fm
E	E	B	F sharp m
F	F	C	Gm
F sharp	F sharp	D flat	A flat m

𝄞 CHAPTER 3: HARMONICA POSITIONS

Scenario 1

You walk into a crowded bar and notice a four-piece blues band rocking out in the corner. You overhear the band leader tell the rest of the band that the next song they will be playing is "The Delta Bad Hand Blues." You happen to know that particular tune on the harmonica. You politely go up to the band leader and ask if you can sit in and play your harmonica with them on that song. He looks at you for a few moments and decides that you've got a pretty honest face, so he asks what key you would like to play it in. You suddenly realize that you only have one harmonica on you and that it is in the key of D. You also know that you like to play that song in second position. Without any hesitation whatsoever, you boldly pronounce that you would like to play it in the key of A. With that quickly out of the way, the band kicks into a four-bar intro and you're off and jamming.

In this scenario the formula that you used looks like this:

Know the key of harmonica + position
= key of song.

Scenario 2

The band enjoyed your playing so much that they invited you back next week. Knowing that you will definitely be sitting in with them, you decide to bring 12 harmonicas, one for each key. Shortly after you arrive they call you to the stage. They ask if you happen to know a particular tune called "Minoring in the Blues." Amazingly, you just learned that one. You know that it's in a minor key and as such you play it in third position. The band leader leans over to let you know that the singer likes to do it in the key of B minor. Again, with no hesitation at all, you reach into your tackle box and pull out a harmonica in the key of A. The song starts. You play the best solo of your life and the crowd goes wild. The band leader makes you a full member of the group right after the set is over. Everyone goes home happy.

In this scenario the formula would look like this:

Know the key of song + position
= key of harmonica.

> **"The song starts. You play the best solo of your life and the crowd goes wild. The band leader makes you a full member of the group right after the set is over. Everyone goes home happy."**

Howlin Wolf on stage with Hubert sumlin at 1815 Club, Chicago, in 1975

Got the idea? As long as you know the position you're playing in plus the key of the song, you can know which harmonica to use. Conversely, if you know the position that you're playing in and the key harmonica that you'll be using, you can tell the band what key to play the song in.

As you start to play along with other people, you'll need to think both ways. Eventually you'll have the more popular keys/positions memorized, but in the meantime the chart on page 81 will help you to figure it out more quickly.

CHAPTER 4
THE DREADED TWO-HOLE DRAW

Question: What's the difference between a good artist and a bad harmonica player?
Answer: A good artist knows how to draw well.

Breathing in (drawing) on certain holes of the harmonica can be a problem for many aspiring harmonica players—a big problem. After playing the fake blues scale in the previous chapter, you might have noticed that the hole-two draw (and maybe other draw notes on the bottom end) aren't responding too well, if at all. They might feel stiff or even stuck. Naturally, you could become very frustrated by this. You might even want to return your harmonica to the store where you purchased it and request a brand new one that actually works. How dare they sell you a broken harmonica? In fact every single harmonica that you've ever purchased (if you have more than one) seems to be broken on the exact same hole, and it's always on a draw note... Hmm... How weird is that?

TIP 1

Some of the sticking occurs when there is too much of a "suction draw." This usually comes from the front part of your mouth. To demonstrate what I mean, put your hand to your mouth and breathe in until you can feel suction. This suction is what you need to eliminate. Try it again, but this time put your hand to your mouth and breathe in from your diaphragm. Think of an "ah" sound as you're doing this. Is all of the suction gone? Keep working at it until all of the suction is eliminated and then try it out on the harmonica over hole two. Keep going back to the hand over the mouth trick until you've assimilated it correctly into your playing with no sticking.

MORE ABOUT THE TWO-HOLE DRAW PROBLEM

Well, there's good news and bad news. The good news is that it's a good bet that your harmonicas are most likely in good working condition. The bad news is that if the problem isn't with the harmonica, then it's most likely with your technique for drawing in. Fear not, this is a very common problem for many people. With a little work, you will master the draw notes at the bottom part of the harmonica. It's a good thing too, because you'll soon see just how expressive and powerful the hole-two draw is.

Whenever you feel the two draw sticking, the harmonica is just trying to let you know that something is amiss with your technique. By learning a few simple tricks, the sticking problems at the bottom of the harmonica will be a thing of the past.

Be patient as you learn to do this. It can take days or weeks before all of the sticking sound is eliminated. After you master this, you'll be able to draw in on hole one, two, and three with total confidence and no resistance at all.

TIP 2

As you place the harmonica in your mouth, make sure you are using the correct embouchure. Try to keep your lips relaxed and lower your bottom jaw. Also, make sure that the harmonica is all the way in your mouth with a relaxed pucker. Your tongue should be at the bottom of your mouth with the tip of it placed on the gum line just below the teeth. Now try breathing in gently from your diaphragm, as you did when you placed your hand to your mouth. If you forgot how the breathing felt while doing that, go back to it with your hand to your mouth. Keep trying to eliminate any suction.

TIP 3

If all else fails, you can temporarily substitute hole-three blow for the hole-two draw. Hole-three blow is the exact same note as hole-two draw, however it's still very important to be able to play the two-hole draw cleanly. It will eventually become one of the most soulful notes that you'll play on the harmonica. It's also a very prominent note that we will be learning to bend down.

♪ CHAPTER 5 ♫
THE BLUES

THIS SECTION:

Wilson Pickett and Dan Aykroyd performing at Madison Square Garden in 1988

𝄞 CHAPTER 5: THE BLUES

You've maybe heard it said that the blues is a feeling, and how true that is. Blues songs stir up strong emotions. A sad blues song might feature lyrics such as "the blues ain't nothin' but a good man feelin' bad" or "the blues ain't nothin' but a woman wanna see her man" or my personal favorite "the blues ain't nothin' but a melted Snickers bar stuck to the dashboard of my new Audi." So, while the blues is indeed a feeling, it's also more than just a feeling.

BLUES BASICS

"The blues" is an art form that contains a variety of musical nuances and unique features. Many of those features are what make us feel what we feel when we hear the blues.

The origin of the blues can be traced back to the nineteenth century—a contentious time in American history. Its originators were slaves, ex-slaves, and descendants of slaves, and the blues grew out of their need to express their struggles and pain. The blues is simple and profound enough that anyone, anywhere, at any time can easily relate to it. This chapter takes a close look at the musical structure of the blues to help you understand how you can make the harmonica relate to it.

During your lifetime you've most likely heard many incarnations of the blues. Much of the popular music of our day (and days past) came directly or indirectly from the blues. Genres such as jazz, rock 'n' roll, country, soul, rap, opera (okay, the last one is a stretch) all evolved from the blues.

One of the more common forms of the blues is called the 12-bar blues. But what are we referring to when we use the word "bar," in "12-bar blues"? Whatever a bar is, we at least know that there are twelve of them, because it says so. But I've been to twelve bars in an evening and felt pretty good, so I'm pretty sure that wasn't the blues.

"The term 'bar,' as it is used here, refers to a measure of music. A measure of music is just a particular amount of time that contains a specific amount of beats or pulses. You can think of a beat as being when your foot taps while listening to a song. The type of 12-bar blues described in this section contains four beats (foot taps) in each measure. "

♪ CHAPTER 5: THE BLUES

Here is a visual representation of the 12-bar blues. Each bar (measure) contains four diagonal hash marks. Each of those hash marks represents a beat (foot tap).

| //// | //// | //// | //// |

| //// | //// | //// | //// |

| //// | //// | //// | //// |

Follow along visually as you listen to *rhythm track # 5-1*. Tap your foot along and count the beats and measures.

The first bar is where the verse (also called a stanza) begins and the last bar is where it ends. When a new verse begins, you go back to bar one. A full 12-bar blues song may contain any amount of verses.

The standard 12-bar blues contains only three basic chords (see page 99). They are often referred to as the "I" (one) chord the "IV" (four) chord, and the "V" (five) chord. We're now going to add in those

chords to specific areas of the 12-bar blues progression. Listen again to the recording on *rhythm track # 5-1*. Start on the first bar. Listen for a change in the music when you see the chord change.

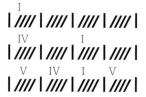

Did you hear it? If not, listen closely a few more times, zeroing in on the bass or the piano.

Now try playing harmonica along with those chords. When you see the I (one) chord, play either hole-two draw or hole-six blow. On the IV (four) chord, play either a hole-one blow or hole-four blow. When you come across the V (five) chord, play either the hole-one draw or hole-four draw.

Listen to the rhythm used with each note on *track # 5-2*. Notice that no matter which of the notes chosen to use at each chord change, the note is always played five times in this particular rhythm. Try to duplicate that same rhythm as you play it on your own along with *rhythm track # 5-1*.

"The blues somehow seems to speak directly to our deepest emotions. That's why we can often relate to a story of struggle and deep pain as we hear the blues being sung."

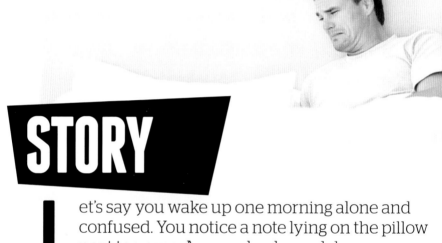

STORY

L et's say you wake up one morning alone and confused. You notice a note lying on the pillow next to yours. As you slowly read down, you realize that your wife (or husband) has left you sometime during the night. You're devastated. To make matters worse, she's drained your entire checking and savings accounts. As you begin to try to make sense of it all, you hear a strange sound coming from the driveway. You peer out of the window, only to witness the back end of your late-model BMW being towed away by the repo man. How could it get any worse than this? The phone rings. You pick up the handset and somehow manage a very deflated-sounding "hello."

It's your boss...

You've overslept for the fourth time this month. Your desk needs to be cleared out by 2pm and your final check is waiting at the front desk. With nowhere to go and no one to turn to, you pick up your faithful old guitar and begin to sing:

My baby up and left me and now I'm out of a job

My baby up and left me and now I'm out of a job

With nowhere left to go, I sit down and begin to sob...

This is a very sad story indeed. It's also a very common form of the blues with which to tell the story. The form used in this song is called an AAB pattern. This pattern fits perfectly over a 12-bar blues progression. The first line (first A) is sung over the first two bars of the song. It informs us of the problem. The second line (second A) is sung over bars five and six and repeats the dilemma, but more emphatically this time. The last line (the B) is sung over bars nine and ten and tells us the response to the problem. The B part also rhymes with the A part. Finally the last two bars are called the turnaround. The turnaround tells your ear that this is the end of this stanza and a new one is about to begin. Voilà, there you have the blues.

PLAYING THE BLUES

One way of playing the harmonica over a 12-bar blues progression is very similar to the way a person (as in the story on the previous page) would sing over a 12-bar blues progression. The first lick (first A part) is played over bars one and two. The next lick (second A part) is repeated and played over bars five and six. Finally the response lick is played over bars nine and ten. Listen to the following licks played over a 12-bar blues on **track # 5-3**. As you listen, follow along by looking at the earlier 12-bar blues diagram. Now try playing it along with the CD. Finally, try it on your own along with **rhythm track # 5-1**.

#5-1

A 4 4 4 4 3 2 4 4 4 4 3 2 2 2

A 4 4 4 4 3 2 4 4 4 4 3 2 2 2

B 4 4 3 4 4 5 4 4 4 4 3 2 2

The Harmonica Boogie

*"The Harmonica Boogie" is a standard tune for all aspiring blues harmonicists (and yes, "harmonicists" is a real word even if my word processor doesn't think so). The melody of the song is also similar to what a bass player might play over a standard 12-bar blues. Listen to it up tempo on **track #5-4**. When you're ready, practice it along with **rhythm track #5-5**.*

#5-5

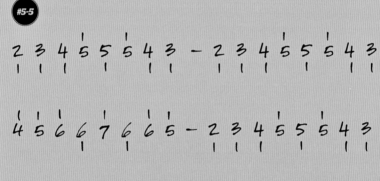

To produce a more "boogie woogie" type of sound, try playing each note twice. As you do, add tongue articulation to each note with a "da" or "ta," just as you did on the comping grooves in Chapter 2. Play the seventh and eighth notes on line three only once. Listen on **track #5-6**. Now try it on your own with **rhythm track #5-5**.

Technical point

A chord consists of three or more notes that, when played simultaneously, harmonize (sound good) together. A major chord consists of the first, third, and fifth notes of the scale. For instance, the notes in a C major scale are:

C, D, E, F, G, A, B

They then resolve back to C in the next octave. If you play the first note of the scale (C), the third note (E), and the fifth note (G) together, you are playing a C major chord.

All of the blow notes on your harmonica, starting at hole one, are the first, third, and fifth notes of the major scale of the key your harmonica is tuned to. For instance, if you have a harmonica in the key of C, all of the blow notes, starting at hole one, are:

C, E, G, C, E, G, C, E, G, C

That's why it sounds good when you blow two or more notes together anywhere on the harmonica. You're automatically playing a chord or part of a chord. It's like built-in music. Your cocker spaniel could even make that sound good, although you probably shouldn't let him play on your harmonica too often.

𝄞 CHAPTER 6 ♫
LICKS, LICKS, AND MORE
LICKS

THIS SECTION:

Victor Deville from
The Acoustic Blues
Company, playing
onstage in Las Palmas,
Canary Islands, Spain

♪ CHAPTER 6: LICKS, LICKS, AND MORE LICKS

Y ou've come to the meat and potatoes of the book. If you've made it this far, give yourself a pat on the back. If you haven't, well... why are you reading this? But, as you're here, you might as well stick around. There're lots of bluesy licks (short musical phrases), songs, and exercises here to help build your musical repertoire. Dig in and enjoy.

CALL AND RESPONSE (SECOND POSITION)

Call and response is a commonly used blues technique to carry on a musical "conversation," usually between two or more separate musicians. The first musician plays a phrase and the second musician answers or plays a response to that phrase, much like a real conversation.

#6-1 ## Call and response exercise

The following exercise contains a call lick with five response licks.
Practice each one first, then try playing them in any order, always alternating
*with the call lick. Listen first to **track # 6-1**.*

#6-2 ## Call lick

2   4   3   3   2

Response lick tracks

#6-3   4   5   4   5   6

#6-4   6   5   4   4   4

#6-5   4   5   6   5   4

#6-6   4   4   3   2   2

#6-7   3   4   4   3   2

TRIPLET LICKS

Earlier we said that every bar (measure) in our 12-bar blues contains four beats (foot taps). Each of these beats is called a quarter note. The next four sets of licks are based on triplets. A triplet is three notes grouped together that together have the same time value (duration) as a quarter note or a foot tap. Since three notes are played in the place of one (quarter) note, triplet licks will go by quickly. For that reason they generally work well with slower tempos. When you feel ready, try them out at a faster tempo as well. They can sound quite impressive.

The first set of licks contains one triplet and one quarter note at the end. Each subsequent set of licks adds in another set of triplets, always ending the lick with a quarter note. All of these licks will be used in different ways and places in the blues progression, depending on the number of triplets in the lick. Listen to each one on the CD first so you can hear how to fit them into the progression. After that, try playing them along with *rhythm track # 6-8*.

A few good triplet licks placed just right can transform an otherwise mediocre solo into something hot... somebody open a window around here!

Two-beat triplet licks
These are played over the first two beats of a measure.

#6-9
4 3 2 – 2

#6-10
4 4 3 – 2

#6-11
5 4 4 – 4

#6-12
6 5 4 – 4

#6-13
3 4 5 – 6

♪ CHAPTER 6: LICKS, LICKS, AND MORE LICKS

Three-beat triplet licks

This next set of triplet licks uses the same first three notes (triplet) as the first set of licks. It then adds a brand new triplet into the mix, ending the lick with a quarter note. These are played over the first three beats of a measure.

#6-14 4 3 2 – 3 4 3 – 2

#6-15 4 4 3 – 4 4 4 – 3

#6-16 5 4 4 – 4 5 4 – 2

#6-17 6 5 4 – 5 4 4 – 4

#6-18 3 4 5 – 5 5 4 – 2

Four-beat triplet licks

These are played over all four beats in a measure.

#6-19 2 3 4 – 4 5 4 – 4 3 2 – 2

#6-20 6 5 4 – 5 4 4 – 4 4 3 – 2

#6-21 4 5 4 – 4 3 4 – 4 4 3 – 2

#6-22 5 4 5 – 6 5 4 – 4 4 3 – 2

#6-23 3 4 5 – 5 5 4 – 3 4 5 – 2

♪ CHAPTER 6: LICKS, LICKS, AND MORE LICKS

Five-beat triplet licks

This last set of triplet licks builds on the previous one by adding another group of triplets into the mix. These are played over a full measure (four beats) plus one beat in the next measure.

#6-24 2 3 4 – 4 5 4 – 4 3 2 – 2 1 2 –

#6-25 6 5 4 – 5 4 4 – 4 4 3 – 4 4 3 – 2

#6-26 4 5 4 4 3 4 4 4 3 4 4 3 2

#6-27 5 4 5 6 5 4 4 4 3 4 3 2 2

#6-28 3 4 5 5 5 4 3 4 5 4 4 3 2

Turnaround licks

*Turnarounds happen on the last two measures of the 12-bar blues. The turnaround
helps our ears to feel a resolution from the verse we've just played and then prepares our
ears to hear a new verse. As such, turnarounds are a very important component of the
blues. Here are three licks that work well over a turnaround.*

#6-29   4 4 4 4 3 2 2 2 — ♪ ♪

#6-30   2 2 3 3 4 4 4 2 — ♪ ♪

#6-31   6 6 5 4 4 4 4 3 2 — ♪ ♪

LIP-SMACKIN' LICKS

Here's another fun technique, called lip smackin', which can produce an endless stream of great licks. You'll also enjoy the grooves this can create when you play them by yourself. These licks contain all of the notes found in the fake blues scale (see page 76).

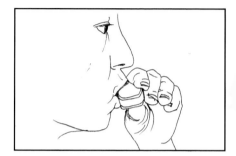

A lip smack is just like the name sounds— a smack (kiss) done with your lips on the harmonica. The main intention is to produce a percussive-sounding "smack" to accompany the note. While lips smacks are not particularly hard to do, it's a good idea to check your sound against the recording (**track # 6-32**).

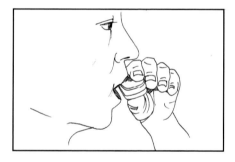

Here's how to produce the lip smack. Try doing this first without the harmonica.

1 Pucker your lips fairly tightly.

2 Using a moderate amount of force, make a kissing (smacking) sound. Try to control your lips so that they move vertically rather than horizontally.

3 After you start to consistently hear a good smacking sound, try it out on the harmonica. Place your lips over hole two using the same embouchure as discussed

earlier (see page 22). Open your mouth vertically during the smack. Finish off the smack with the top of the harmonica still touching your upper lip but the bottom of the harmonica completely free of the bottom lip.

4 The emphasis should be on the percussive smack rather than the actual note it produces. Listen to the CD and try to duplicate the sound. After you're comfortable getting the smack on hole two, try it out on holes one, three, and four.

"This is a great exercise to practice while you're stopped at a traffic light... and everyone is watching!"

♪ CHAPTER 6: LICKS, LICKS, AND MORE LICKS

Lip-smackin' grooves

Following are five very hip lip smackin' grooves. Each lick "smacks" on a different beat. This helps to create a different feel for each one. The numbers under the licks (on page 114) represent which beat to play that particular note on. The downbeat happens when you tap your foot down. The downbeat can land on any of the four beats in a measure (1, 2, 3, or 4). The plus sign represents the "and" or "upbeat." That's when your foot is coming up. A note may fall on either the downbeat or the upbeat. It's not as hard as it may sound—to help, on the CD, each of these licks is played in the left channel and the count ("one and two and three and four and") in the right channel.

We're going to insert the lip smack at different places on each lick (e.g. beat 1, beat 2, and so on) to produce a variety of sounds.

Practice these licks in the order in which they're listed, as they will get progressively harder. After you've mastered them, try playing them one after another, mixing up the order each time through.

Lip-smackin' music notation

' = smack on hole one   " = smack on hole two
"' = smack on hole three   "" = smack on hole four

Lip-smackin' exercise

The following lip smackin' exercise is a fun one to get you started. It works well over a 12-bar blues. You'll be smackin' on holes one and two. On this exercise, insert the smack on beats two and four. Listen first to **track # 6-33**, *then play along.*

```
2  "   123  123  "       2  "   123  123  "
↓      ↓↓↓  ↓↓↓           ↓      ↓↓↓  ↓↓↓

2  "   123  123  "       2  "   123  123  "
↓      ↓↓↓  ↓↓↓           ↓      ↓↓↓  ↓↓↓

↓  ♪ ↓↓ ♪   ↓  ♪ ↓↓ ♪    2  "   123  123  "
↓     ↓↓     ↓     ↓↓ ♪   ↓      ↓↓↓  ↓↓↓
```

Call and response lip smack

This time you're going to use the same "call" lick from earlier in the chapter (see page 103), but the response is going to include a lip smack. This makes for a real nice groove.

#6-34 **Theme lick**

```
    ↑  ↑
2  4  3  3  2  "   123  123
↓      ↓  ↓      ↓↓↓  ↓↓↓
```

#6-35 Smacks on the "and" of beat 1

2   ,,   3 2 2 | 2 | 2   ,,   3 2 2 | 2 | etc...

1 + 2 + 3 + 4 +   1 + 2 + 3 + 4 +

#6-36 Smacks on the "and" of beat 2

| | 2   ,,   3 2 2 | | | 2   ,,   3 2 2 | etc...

1 + 2 + 3 + 4 +   1 + 2 + 3 + 4 +

#6-37 Smacks on the "and" of beat 3

| | 2 | 2   ,,   2 | | | 2 | 2   ,,   2 | etc...

1 + 2 + 3 + 4 +   1 + 2 + 3 + 4 +

#6-38 Smacks on the "and" of beat 4

3 2 2 | | | 2   ,,   3 2 2 | | | 2   ,, etc...

1 + 2 + 3 + 4 +   1 + 2 + 3 + 4 +

#6-39 Smacks on beat 1 and on the "and" of 3

,   2 2 | 2   ,,   2 | ,   2 2 | 2   ,,   2 | etc...

1 + 2 + 3 + 4 +   1 + 2 + 3 + 4 +

The following two songs are each 12-bar blues featuring a number of lip smacks inserted on a variety of different beats. The second one is a bit more challenging than the first one. Listen to each one first, then play them along with **rhythm track # 6-40**.

After you can play each one separately, try playing them together one after another.

"Research from a recent harmonica smackin' study found that 92 percent of the participants showed considerable improvement in their kissing techniques and abilities. Most of their spouses were literally begging them to practice (a lot more). So... smack often and be proud of it."

Lip-smackin' blues #1
#6-41
Second position

1st chorus

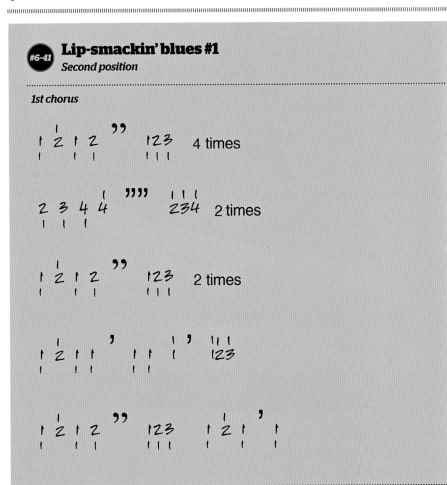

#6-42 Lip-smackin' blues #2

Second position

♪ CHAPTER 6: LICKS, LICKS, AND MORE LICKS

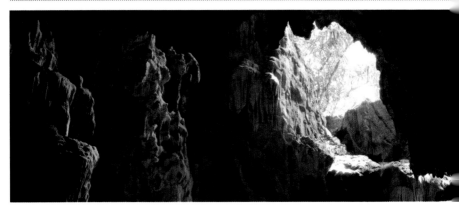

THE FLINTSTONES BLUES—12-BAR BLUES IN SECOND POSITION

Our next 12-bar blues is a culmination of some of the licks and ideas that we've been building on in this and also the previous chapter. Think of the melody in this next song as a conversation between two people: Fred and his wife, Wilma. Refer to the song below as you hear a short description of their conversation.

Conversation

When the very first I (one) chord is sounded, Fred starts to talk to Wilma about a problem he's having with his best friend Barney. As he's telling her about it his frustration begins to grow, so he repeats it to Wilma (second line), only this time with a slight variation.

As the IV chord is being played, Wilma responds to Fred's problem by telling him that he's always complaining about some kind of problem with Barney, and why doesn't he (Fred) just grow up? Fred, as usual, isn't listening to Wilma. During the next I chord (fourth line), Fred interrupts Wilma and starts to complain about Barney yet again. By the time we get to the V chord, Wilma has had enough. She's tired of Fred always ignoring her. She tells Fred that she's packing her bags and heading over to her mother's house. On the turnaround (last two measures), Fred looks up at Wilma with a clueless expression and replies: "Were you just talking to me?" And there you have it.

#6-43 Fred's problem

*As you listen to the song on **track # 6-43**, try to hear the dialog. Even if you don't hear Fred and Wilma, you'll still have a yabba dabba do good time playing the song.*

I chord

4 4 4 4 3 2   4 4 4 4 3

(problem repeated)

4 4 4 4 3 4 5 4 5 5 4 3 2

IV chord
(Wilma's response)

ı ı ((4 4 4 3 2   ı ı ((4 4 4 3 2

I chord
(Fred states his problem again and interrupts Wilma)

4 4 4 4 3 4 5 4 5 5 4 3 2

V chord
(Wilma's mad!)

ı   4 3 4 4

IV chord
(Wilma's leaving)

ı   4 4 4 3 2 2 2

Turnaround

(Fred's clueless)

3 2 3   4 3 4   4 4 3 2 ı ı

Triplet   Triplet

119

CHAPTER 6: LICKS, LICKS, AND MORE LICKS ♫

Playing dirty

Another technique that can be used to get a grittier sound on the Flintstones Blues, or any blues song, is referred to as "playing dirty."

As the name implies, it's the exact opposite of playing clean. For the moment, forget everything that you've learned about getting clean single notes. Now you're going to go for sloppy notes, or more specifically two or three notes at a time. Certain combinations of notes played together sound better than others, but any combination of adjacent holes will work. Listen to the Flintstones Blues again, but this time listen out for a dirty sound on **track # 6-44**.

When the melody's being played on hole-four draw, the hole-five draw is also played simultaneously. Whenever the melody's played on hole-three draw, the hole-four draw is played simultaneously. When you're playing dirty, you don't necessarily have to make every note dirty; just mix up the dirty notes with some clean notes as well. Listen to the dirty version of the Flintstones Blues a few times, then try your own dirty version. Just make sure to clean up for dinner...

THIRD-POSITION FAKE BLUES SCALE

Third position works very well for the blues. The difference between playing the blues in second position and third position is that third-position blues is usually played as a minor blues. Before you learn a minor blues song in third position, let's learn the fake blues scale in third position. The proper musical term for this is a minor pentatonic scale. Listen to what it sounds like on ***track # 6-45***.

4 5 6 6 7 8

Definition
Just as a pentagon has five sides, the pentatonic scale contains five notes in each octave. A short and succinct scale, but very musical.

#6-46 Minor blues, third position

This 12-bar minor blues song uses all of the notes found in the third-position minor pentatonic scale. The play-along track has a nice calypso groove to it (rhythm track # 6-47).

4 – 6 5 6 5 4 4 4 4 5 6

4 – 6 5 6 5 4 4 4 4 5 6

6 6 5 6 6 6 5   6 6 5 6 6 6 5

4 – 6 5 6 5 4 4 4 4 5 6

6 6 5 6 6   8 8 7 6 6 5

4 – 6 5 6 5 4 4 4 4 5 6

♪ CHAPTER 6: LICKS, LICKS, AND MORE LICKS

#6-48 **#6-49** ## St. James Infirmary Blues

*"St. James Infirmary Blues" (**track 6-48**), first recorded in 1928 by the great Louis Armstrong, is a standard in the blues genre. This minor melody works well in third position and uses many of the same notes found in the third-position fake blues scale (see page 122). Play along on **rhythm track # 6-49**.*

4	5	6	6	6	6	6	5	4		4	5	6	6	8	7	6

4 5 6 6 6 6 6 5 4   8 7 6 6 5 4 4 4

124

Louis Armstrong

Having fun so far? I certainly hope so. In the next chapter, you're going to take things up a notch as you learn to bend notes. Good technique (breathing, embouchure, etc...) is going to play a huge role in note bending, so if you need to brush up a bit, this is a good time to do it.

When you're all set, take a deep breath and turn the page... Just make sure to exhale at some point...

𝄞 CHAPTER 7 ♪

BENDING THE BLUES

THIS SECTION:

♪ CHAPTER 7: BENDING THE BLUES

THE DESIGN OF THE HARMONICA

Everything you've learned to play up to this point has been played with notes that can be produced by blowing and drawing. In this chapter you are going to learn how to produce notes that are available by using a technique different than simply blowing and drawing. These notes are called bent notes and they play a huge role in achieving the sought after "bluesy" sound that the harmonica is so well known for. You'll discover the original intent behind the design of the harmonica, what a bent note is, which notes can be bent, and the techniques involved in bending. Then there is a short section about the physics behind bent notes. There are also lots of great bending exercises along with some cool tunes that feature bent notes. So, if you're all set, let's get started.

The harmonica was invented in Germany in the mid-1800s. The original intention behind its design was to play German folk songs and other simple melodies. Most of these types of melodies were, and still are, played in the middle octave of the harmonica where all of the notes in the major scale (white piano keys) are located. The first and third octaves of the harmonica do not contain all of the notes found in the major scale so many melodies cannot be played there. However, the first and third octaves do contain all of the notes needed to play the chords that can accompany a simple melody. Listen to an example on *track # 7-1*.

The piano diagram on page 130 represents the notes on a piano laid out over the same range (three octaves) as a harmonica in the key of C. All of the black keys, along with the grayed-out white keys, are notes that can't be played on the harmonica by just blowing out and drawing in. The original intent and design of the harmonica never allowed for these notes to be sounded. However, as we shall soon see, an incredible paradigm shift happened, allowing these formerly missing notes to be produced. Somebody, somewhere in time, accidentally discovered what we now refer to on a harmonica as bent notes. To get a clearer picture of this, let's first back up a bit..

TECHNICAL STUFF

As mentioned earlier, there are 12 notes contained in the range of one octave. The first octave on the harmonica starts at hole-one blow and goes up to the hole-three draw (C to B). The second octave starts at hole-four blow and goes up to the hole-seven draw (C to B). The third octave starts at the hole-seven blow and goes to what is called a "blow bend" on hole ten (more on blow bends later). Finally, there is one note left (C) on the hole-ten blow.

Ok, ready for some math? Twelve notes in an octave multiplied by three octaves (range on the harmonica) gives us 36 notes. Adding in the last C note on the ten-hole blow brings that number up to a grand total of 37 notes. It's amazing to think that this little instrument has such a wide range of notes.

All of this is fine until you consider that there are only ten holes on the harmonica and only two notes can be played in each hole (blowing and drawing). Using this combination provides a possible 20 notes. To make matters worse, remember that the hole-two draw and hole-three blow are the same note (both are G notes). So, there are actually only 19 possible notes that can be played over a 37-note range.

Whew... that's a lot to digest. Maybe this next story will help you to understand all of this in a more practical way.

> *"Someone, somewhere in time accidentally discovered what we now refer to as bent notes. This allows us to now play many of the formerly inaccessible notes on a harmonica. Twelve notes in an octave multiplied by three octaves (range on the harmonica) gives us 36 notes. Adding in the last C note on the ten-hole blow brings that number up to a grand total of 37 notes."*

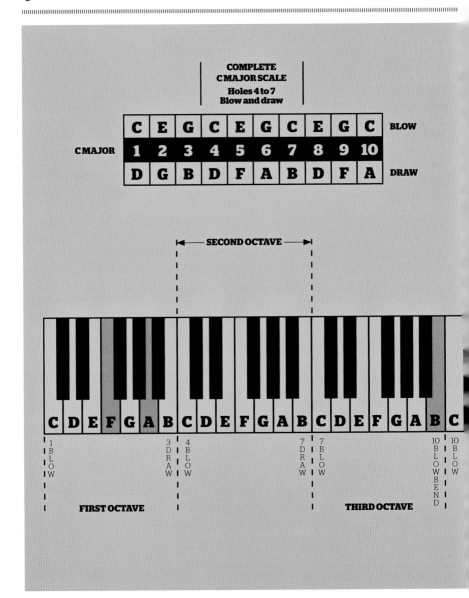

STORY

Imagine that the year is 1745. You are hosting a dinner party for some friends. Your honored guest for the evening is none other than the world-renowned pianist/composer, Johann Sebastian Bach. Soon after dinner is finished, some of your guests request a short performance from Mr. Bach.

Fortunately, you happen to have a small three-octave piano (36 notes plus a note on the very top) sitting in the next room. Unfortunately, you are totally unaware that your four-year-old daughter has spilled her orange pudding, a cinnamon scone, and a box of French macaroons inside the piano. You politely excuse yourself to prepare the piano for the performance. To your horror, you realize that 18 of the 37 notes on the piano aren't working at all. That's almost half of them. Only 19, seemingly random, notes can be

sounded, but it's too late. The guests have begun taking their seats.

"Air on a G String" from Bach's third orchestral suite in D major is quickly requested. Mr. Bach takes his seat at the bench in front of the piano. A hushed tone falls over the crowd. Your stomach begins to churn. As the music slowly begins, it quickly becomes apparent that something is terribly wrong. Has Johann had too much wine? Are his skills beginning to diminish? It slowly starts to dawn on Bach that only the very simplest of melodies can be performed in just the middle octave of this very limited piano. With that new information in mind, Bach begins tinkering with a brand new melody he hears in his head. It's a much simpler melody than any other he's composed before. It sounds vaguely familiar... While you don't realize it at the time, your dinner party has dramatically changed the course of music history. Johann Sebastian Bach (not Stephen Foster) is now credited with the song "Oh Susannah." Only Bach's most loyal fans are moved by this new composition, especially the "banjo on my knee" section.

Sad to say, this is kind of how it is (or was) with the harmonica, until bent notes came along...

♪ CHAPTER 7: BENDING THE BLUES

WHAT ARE BENT NOTES?

A bent note is any note that has been lowered in pitch by employing a specific method(s) that involves the tongue, breathing, and your vocal cavity. A draw bend is a note that has been lowered in pitch and is produced by drawing in, specifically on holes one, two, three, four, or six. Draw bending can produce up to eight of the 18 missing notes on five holes of the harmonica (see diagram).

A blow bend is a bent note that has been lowered in pitch and is produced by blowing out, specifically on holes eight, nine, or ten. Blow bending can produce four more of the missing notes on three holes of the harmonica (see diagram). Using a combination of draw bends and blow bends, 12 of the 18 missing notes can be played. The other six missing notes can be achieved by using two techniques, known as "over-blowing" and "over-drawing." Both over-blowing and over-drawing are advanced techniques recently popularized—in the last 20 years—and used by a growing number of present-day harmonica players. Using a combination of all four of these techniques, the full note range (all 37 notes) on a diatonic harmonica can be played. Pretty cool,

huh? Though it's still probably best to keep scones and orange pudding far away from your harmonica...

Over the years, all of these "missing notes" were discovered through trial, experiment, or by accident. None of them was ever intended to be part of the original harmonica sound. It was all just a crazy (good) accident waiting to happen.

When considering each of these four techniques for the beginning harmonica player, draw bending is by far the most important for achieving that highly emotive, bluesy sound. As such, that's what you'll learn in the rest of this chapter. First, listen to what a draw bend sounds like on ***track # 7-2***.

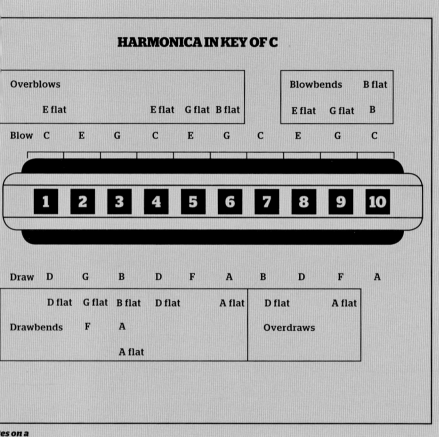

HARMONICA IN KEY OF C

Overblows						**Blowbends**		**B flat**	
	E flat			E flat	G flat	B flat	E flat	G flat	B
Blow	C	E	G	C	E	G	C	E	G	C

| 1 | 2 | 3 | 4 | 5 | 6 | 7 | 8 | 9 | 10 |

Draw	D	G	B	D	F	A	B	D	F	A
	D flat	G flat	B flat	D flat		A flat	D flat		A flat	
Drawbends		F	A				**Overdraws**			
			A flat							

tes on a
rmonica in
e key of C

CHAPTER 7: BENDING THE BLUES

Which draw notes can be bent?

As discussed, holes one, two, three, four, and six can all produce draw bends. Some of those holes are capable of producing more than one bent note. The rule is that the highest pitched note in each hole (either the blow or the draw) can be bent down to produce whatever note or notes are found between that and the lowest note in the hole.

For example, let's look at hole one as we refer to the harmonica diagram on page 133 and the piano diagram on page 130. The blow note in hole one is a C and the draw note is a D. Since D is the higher of the two notes and also a draw note, it can be draw bent down to produce a D flat note, which is the note between C and D. If you look at hole two, G is the draw note and a higher-pitched note than the blow note (E). It can therefore be draw bent down to an F sharp and also an F, which are the two notes found between E and G.

Hole three can produce three draw-bent notes (B flat, A, and A flat). Hole four is the same as hole one, but one octave up. It can therefore produce one bent note, a D flat. Hole six can produce one bent note, an A flat. Hole five can be bent down slightly, but not actually to another pitch. That's because it contains an E as a blow note and an F as a draw note. Since there are no pitches found between E and F, there is not a note to bend to on hole five.

Harmonicas of different keys will produce different notes when bent; however, they will all be the same proportionally. Hole two always has two draw bends, hole three always has three bends, hole four will always have one bend etc. As such, whatever you play on one harmonica is played in the same way on a differently keyed harmonica; it will just end up in a different key.

TECHNIQUES FOR BENDING

Learning to bend notes and make them sound good takes time. Be patient and tenacious with your practice. It could take weeks before you get your first bend, and take months to get them all and play them in tune.

The mouth, tongue, and vocal cavity differ slightly from person to person. This means the techniques for using them to produce bent notes will also differ slightly from person to person. Below are some tips and suggestions on how to produce draw bends. It's your job to experiment with them to see what works best for you.

Draw bends

Redirecting the air flowing into the mouth produces all bent notes. One of the best ways to redirect airflow is to use the tongue.

1 Whistle while breathing in; notice where your tongue is positioned as you're doing this. It should be somewhere close to the center of your mouth. If you're unable to make a whistling sound as you breathe in, that's okay. Just listen to the sound of the air as it's passing into your mouth while trying to make a soft "whee" sound.

Fabio Treves of Treves Blues Band, Brescia, Italy,2008

2 While still whistling in with a "whee" sound, change your tongue position as though you were going to produce a "yo" sound. As you do this, your tongue should be moving back and downward inside your mouth. You may not actually hear a "whee" or "yo" sound, but you will hear changes in the sound of the passing air as your tongue shifts to a new position. To make the sound more pronounced, take your index finger and place it gently on your lips and try "whee" and "yo" again. The way that your tongue moves as you do this is very much like the way it moves when bending a note. Let's try a few more variations.

3 This time, start with an "ah" sound before switching to a "yo" sound. Moving from "ah" to "yo" will produce a slightly different sound than "whee" to "yo."

4 Now start with a "ka" sound and go to a "yoo" sound. The "ka" should feel more pronounced in your throat than it did starting with the "whee" or the "ah." Could you hear the sound of the air change as the sounds changed?

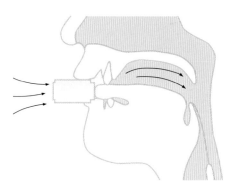

5 Try these again, but this time visualize your airstream as you change sounds. Can you feel the air hitting the roof of your mouth as you change sounds? When your tongue shifts position, the airflow between your tongue and the roof of your mouth narrows. This creates an air tunnel, which is good, just what we're looking for.

Now let's try it out on the harmonica over hole one. This is usually the easiest bend to get first.

6 First, listen to ***track # 7-3*** to hear what hole one bent down should sound like. Next, place your mouth over hole one making sure that you have a good, airtight seal and are using the correct embouchure (see page 22). Start with an "ah" sound. Breathe it in gently for a few seconds and then go to the "yo" sound. Did anything happen? If not, no problem, it takes time. Try it again while making sure to keep your breathing relaxed.

This time as you go to the "yo" sound, drop your jaw slightly. You won't need to when bending on any of the other holes, but it helps a bit on hole one. It also helps if you can hear the bend in your head. For this reason you'll want to go back and listen to the recording fairly often, even after you've got your bend. In general, when first learning to bend, some holes are definitely harder than others. Here is a suggested order for learning them. Again, everyone is different, so experiment.

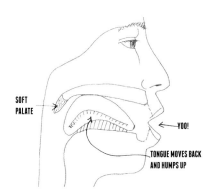

SOFT PALATE

YOO!

TONGUE MOVES BACK AND HUMPS UP

7 After you've managed to get hole one to bend, try it out on hole four (***track # 7-4***). As you attempt to draw bend on the higher holes (four and six), start with a "whee" and then switch your second sound to more closely resemble the "yoo."

REMEMBER: Different bends on different holes will require different mouth shapes.

8 Finally, let's try holes two and three. These will provide even more of a challenge as they each contain multiple bends. Go back to a "yo" sound for these lower-pitched holes. The first bend (F sharp) on hole two will be closer to a "yoo" shape while changing over to "yo" for the second bend (***track # 7-5***). Hole three will have more of a "ye" shape on the first bend, moving to a "yoo" for the second bend, and finally to "yo" for the third bend (***track # 7-6***). Remember, everyone is different so don't be afraid to experiment.

The most important thing to remember when bending notes on a harmonica is to not try too hard: think, "finesse not force." Bending notes is a rather gentle technique that requires conscious effort. There is a real method to it, not a "muscle up" approach. If a note doesn't bend right away (and it won't), resist the urge to draw harder.

After you become more comfortable bending notes down from an open note (eg D to D flat), you'll want to learn how to start directly on a bent note. Finally you'll want to practice going from bent note to bent note while keeping the pitches in tune. A good way to practice that is to play the bent note on the harmonica while simultaneously hitting the same note on a piano or keyboard and adjusting the pitch of the bent note whenever necessary.

> *"When it comes to bending notes, always think finesse, not force."*

𝄞 CHAPTER 7: BENDING THE BLUES

THE SCIENCE OF BENDING

As mentioned earlier, when we bend a note, we're redirecting the airflow into our mouth and throat. To better understand why a note will bend when we do this, let's first take a look at what's happening inside the harmonica.

The way a harmonica produces a sound is actually quite simple. Inside the harmonica are small strips of metal called reeds (refer to the diagram on page 191). The reeds are riveted onto a flat metal plate called a reed plate. There are two reeds in each hole (chamber). One is above the chamber and is used for blow notes and the other one is below the chamber and is used for draw notes. As you breathe into a hole, air passes over the appropriate reed (blow or draw), causing it to vibrate. The number of times a reed vibrates per second determines the pitch of the note. Each reed is a different length (and weight) and therefore vibrates at a different speed. Pretty simple, right? Not so fast...

Bent notes (as well as over-blown notes) are actually produced by the interaction of the blow and draw reeds with one another.

Let's say that you are bending hole four. As you draw in, the draw reed on hole four begins to vibrate at its predetermined speed producing a D note. When you employ the proper bending techniques (above), the draw reed begins to curve slightly upward toward the blow reed at the top of the chamber. The blow reed in hole four literally "catches wind" of this and begins to vibrate sympathetically with the draw reed. The further the draw reed curves up, the more the blow reed begins to vibrate until eventually the draw reed stops sounding and almost all of the sound (the new D flat note) is being produced by the blow reed. All of this happens in an instant.

How did something so simple become so complicated? Over the course of many years bending has evolved until it's now become an integral part of harmonica playing.

Reed response to blowing out

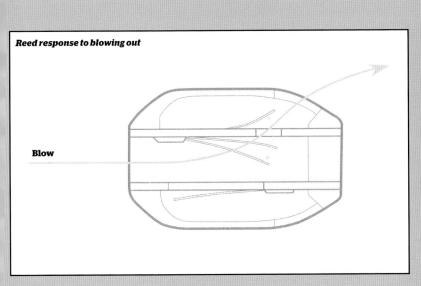

Blow

Reed response to drawing in

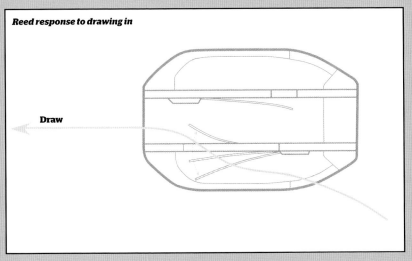

Draw

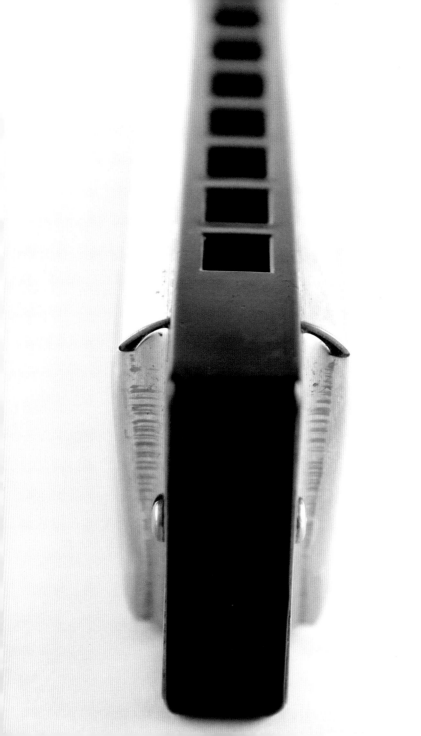

CHAPTER 7: BENDING THE BLUES

The bottom line

There are lots of reasons to become proficient at bending notes on the harmonica. Two of the most important reasons are:

1 More notes will be available to you. That means you'll be able to play many more songs and licks that would otherwise not have been possible.

2 Bent notes deliver a uniquely emotive sound. They can take on the expressive quality of a human voice "moanin'" the blues. They truly are the heart and sould of the harmonica.

Draw bending exercises

As you learn to bend notes on different holes of the harmonica, use the following exercises (see overleaf, where applicable) to strengthen your bent notes on that particular hole.

"Bent notes are truly the heart and soul of the harmonica."

#7-7 **Hole one**

#7-8 **Hole two/first bend**

#7-9 **Hole two/second bend**

#7-10 **Hole three/first bend**

#7-11 Hole three/second bend

```
3⌢  3⌢ 3      4 3⌢  3⌢ 3      2 3⌢  3⌢ 3      3⌢ 3 4
1   ‡   1      1 1   ‡   1      1 1   ‡   1      ‡   1 1

4 3⌢ 3 2
1 ‡  1 1
```

#7-12 Hole four

```
4⌢ 4⌢ 4       4⌢ 4 4́       5 4⌢ 4⌢ 4       4⌢ 4 3
1  +  1       1  +          1 1  +  1       1  + 1

4́ 4⌢ 4
  + 1
```

#7-13 Hole six

```
6⌢ 6⌢ 6       6⌢ 6⌢ 6́       5 6⌢ 6⌢ 6       6́ 6⌢ 6
1  +  1       1  +           1 1  +  1         + 1
```

SECOND POSITION REAL BLUES SCALE

In Chapter 6, you learned the "fake" blues scale and also some songs that were based on that scale. Now that you can bend notes, you're ready for the real blues scale. The fake blues scale opened up new doors for you, but the real blues scale is going to open up new worlds.

G Bb C Db D F G *(track # 7-14)*

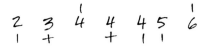

Practice this scale up and down, forward and backward, until you have it mastered and memorized. When you do, try jamming with it on ***rhythm track # 7-15***. Use the same method to jam with it as you did on the one-note blues jam in Chapter 3 (see page 78).

1 Start with one note in the blues scale. Hole-four draw is a good one to start with.

2 Add a nice rhythm to it and play along with the rhythm track.

3 Next, add another note, maybe the hole-four bend this time, and jam along.

4 Keep adding notes from the blues scale, one at a time. You'll gradually begin to feel more comfortable improvising over the full scale. Remember that space (as in, leaving some between the notes) is a good thing.

5 Work on the following licks. Gradually add them into your playing as you continue jamming along with the rhythm track.

#7-16

6 5 4 ⌒ 4 4 3 2
    1   +   + 1

#7-17

4 ⌒ 4 ⌒ 4 5 4 5 6
1   +   1 1 1 1

#7-18

4 ⌒ 4 ⌒ 4 4 3 2 2
1   +   1   + 1 1

#7-19

4 ⌒ 4 5 4 ⌒ 4 3 2
+   1 1 1   + + 1

#7-20

3 4 4 4 3 2 2
+   +   + 1 1

Extended blues scale

If we were to extend the blues scale by going higher, past hole six, we'd find that some of the notes in it are unavailable without the use of over blows and over draws. However, the scale can be extended downward to the hole-one blow, at which point we run out of notes (holes). As you do this, notice that some of the notes from the blues scale end up being on really juicy bent notes. Listen to it going up first and then back down on **track # 7-21**. Now, try playing it, starting on hole six and going down. Once you're able to do that cleanly, then try starting at hole one and going up.

C	Db	D	F	G	Bb	C	Db	D	F	G
\						(				\
(	ı	ı	2	2	3	4	4	4	5	6
	+	ı	≠	ı	+		+	ı	ı	

Extended blues scale in triplets

This is an excellent, challenging exercise to help you master the extended blues scale. In this exercise, the scale will be played in triplets. It starts on hole six and is played through completely, up and down, three times. The tricky part is that each time through, the notes will land in different places in the triplet. For example, look at the hole-six blow (ringed). The first time through the scale, the hole-six blow is played on the first note in the triplet. The second time

through, the hole-six blow lands on the third note in the triplet. The last time through, the hole-six blow is played on the second note in the triplet. As you practice, try to emphasize the first note in each triplet. Also, make sure to keep the bent notes in tune. Go very slow at first, trying to play as cleanly as possible. When you feel ready, gradually pick up the tempo. Once you've got this mastered, you are truly ready for prime time.

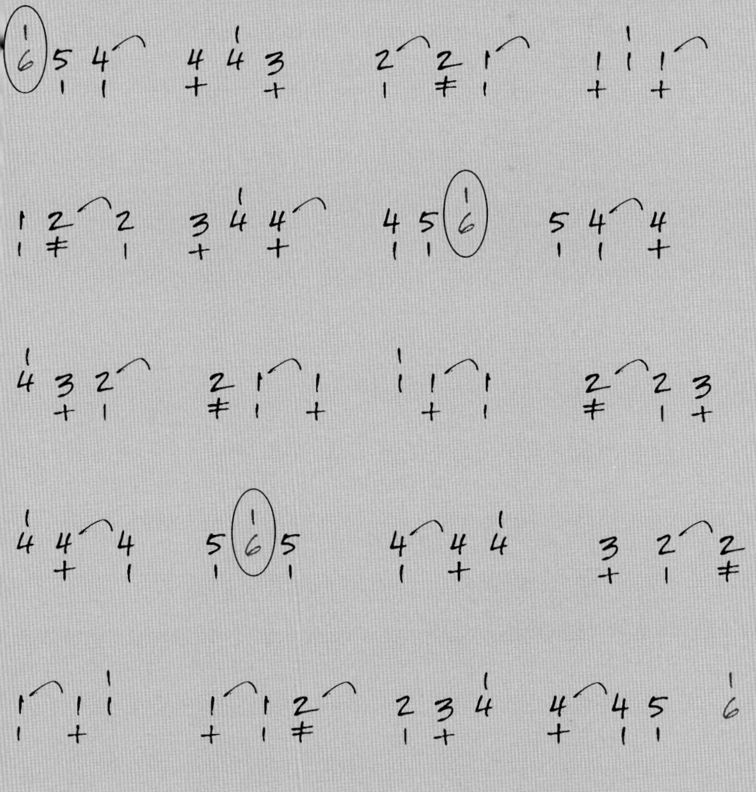
6 5 4 4 4 3 2 2 1 1 1 1
1 2 2 3 4 4 4 5 6 5 4 4
4 3 2 2 1 1 1 1 1 2 2 3
4 4 4 5 6 5 4 4 4 3 2 2
1 1 1 1 1 2 2 3 4 4 4 5 6

♂ CHAPTER 7: BENDING THE BLUES

Extended blues scale licks

#7-23

```
 4⌢ 4  4  3  2⌢ 2⌢ 2
 ↓  +  +  ↓  ≠     ↓
```

#7-24

```
 2⌢ 2  ↑⌢ ↑⌢  ↑  2⌢ 2
 ↓  ≠  ↓  +   ↓  ≠   ↓
```

#7-25

```
 ↑  2⌢ 2⌢ 2  ↑ ↑↑
 ↓  ≠  ↓  ≠  ↓ ↓↓
```

#7-26

```
 3  4  3  2⌢ 2  ↑ 2
 +  +  ↓  ≠  ↓  ↓ ↓
```

#7-27

```
 2⌢ 2  3  2⌢ 2  ↑ 2
 ≠  ↓  +  ↓  ≠  ↓ ↓
```

The Harmonica Boogie (with bends)

Remember "The Harmonica Boogie" that we played earlier? This is a more advanced version that includes some nice bends in the melody. Start slowly and try to get a clear distinction in the pitches on the second and third bends on hole three.

```
  2  3  4  5  5  5  4  3      2  3  4  5  5  5  4  3
  I  I  I     I     I  I      I  I  I     I     I  I


  1  2  3  3   3   3  2  2     2  3  4  5  5  5  4  3
              ≠   +   ≠  I     I  I  I     I     I  I


  1  2  3   3   1  2  3  3     2  3  4  4   4  4  3   3
  I  +  ≠   I            ≠     I  I     +   I  I  ≠
```

Third-position real blues scale

The third-position real blues scale is an easy transition from the fake third-position blues scale (see page 76). All you'll need to do is add one note. That happens to be the hole-six bend. Play it in both directions until it feels comfortable.

D	F	G	Ab	A	C	D

4   5   6   6   6   7   8
                +

"Much of the juiciest blues in third position happens right in the middle part of the harmonica."

The following licks are based on the third-position blues scale. Try playing them along with the rhythm track we used for the minor blues in Chapter 6, **rhythm track # 6-47**.

#7-30

8   7   6⌢   6   6   5   4   4   4
| | + | | |

#7-31

6⌢   6   6   5   4   4   4   5   4
| + | | | | |

#7-32

4   5   6   6   6   5   4   4   4
| | + | | |

#7-33

6   6   7   6   6   5   4   5   4
| + | | | | |

#7-34

6   6   7   6   6   5   4   4   4
+ | + | | |

Comin' Home Baby

"Comin' Home Baby" is a standard in any blues repertoire. It was written and first recorded in the early sixties by legendary composer and vocalist Mel Tormé. The melody works out nicely in both second and third position. Here are both versions.

#7-35 **Third position** *Rhythm track # 7-36*

```
              |              |
4  5  6  –  4  5  6  6  5  4  4  4–5
|  |  |     |  |  |     |  |     |  |

       |              |        |
4  5  6  –  4  5  6  6  5  4  4  4–5
|  |        |  |  |     |  |     |  |

              |
4  5  6  –  6  6  5  4
|  |  |     +     |  |
```

#7-37 **Second position** *Rhythm track # 7-38*

```
                   |
2  3  4  –  2  3  4  4  3  2⌢2⌢2  3
|  +  |     |  +  |     +  |   ≠   |  +

       |              |
2  3  4  –  2  3  4  4  3  2⌢2⌢2  3
|  +        |  +  |     +  |   ≠   |  +

              |
2  3  4  –  4  4  3  2
|  +  |     +     +  |
```

Summertime (third position)

*The tune "Summertime" was composed by George Gershwin for the 1935 opera "Porgy and Bess." Since that time it's gone on to become a jazz standard. Keeping the second bend on hole three in tune is a nice challenge. Listen to it on **track # 7-39**. Practice it along with **rhythm track # 7-40**.*

#7-39 **Summertime (third position)** *rhythm track # 7-40*

6 5 6   6 5 6 6 5 4 3   6 5 6 5 4 5 4
↓ ↓ ↓   ↓ ↓   ↓ ↓ ↓ ₮   ↓ ↓   ↓ ↓ ↓ ↓

6 5 6   6 5 6 6 5 4 3
↓ ↓ ↓   ↓ ↓   ↓ ↓ ↓ ₮

4 4 4 5 6 ⌒ 6 7 6 6 5 4 4
↓ ↓   ↑ +   ↓ ↓ ↓ ↓ ↓ ↓

♪ CHAPTER 7: BENDING THE BLUES

BLOW BENDING

There's good news and there's bad news. The bad news is that blow bending is yet another technique to learn on the harmonica. The good news is that it's usually not nearly as difficult to learn as draw bending. The even better news is that blow bends can be just as expressive, impressive, and fun to play as the draw bends. As if all of that weren't enough, blow bending allows you to access four more pitches for your ever-growing arsenal of harmonica notes. Refer to the harmonica diagram on page 133 to identify those four notes, found on holes eight, nine, and ten.

Blow bending occurs at the high end of the harmonica and things can feel a little dark and mysterious when you get up there.

Here's the reason: The highest note in each of the holes, one through six, is on the draw note. Starting with hole seven, things are reversed and now the highest note in each hole is on the blow note. It might not seem like much of a difference, but playing on holes seven through ten is a very different experience than playing on holes one through six. For this reason, many harmonica players tend to neglect the high end of the instrument. That's too bad, because the high end of the harmonica is just as exciting as the low end. One of the main reasons for that is because of the blow bends. While draw bending helps to create the emotion, blow bending adds to the excitement.

John Popper of
Blues Traveler

🎼 CHAPTER 7: BENDING THE BLUES

The easiest way to learn to blow bend is by practicing it on a lower-key harmonica such as a G or an A. The reeds on lower-key harmonicas are longer and more flexible, making them more suitable for the beginner blow bender. If you don't have access to a lower-key harmonica, fear not, ultimately, the same technique will work on any harmonica; it might just take a wee bit longer to learn. Whether you are draw bending or blow bending, always remember the golden rule: Finesse not force.

Following are a few tips and tricks to help you to achieve the blow bends.

Once you are able to get the note bent down, try to feel the pressure inside your mouth as your tongue shifts forward and downward. Controlling that pressure with your tongue will allow you to control and release the bend cleanly. Your blow bends will be on hole eight (E flat), hole nine (G flat), the first bend on hole ten (B), and then the second bend on hole ten (B flat). As you move up the harmonica from hole eight, the pea-sized opening at the front of your mouth will gradually get smaller.

On the following tracks each bend will be played on a G harmonica first and then played on a C harmonica:
Blow bend on hole eight: ***track # 7-41***
Blow bend on hole nine: ***track # 7-42***
Blow bend on hole ten: ***track # 7-43***

TIP 1
Cover over hole eight with your mouth making sure that you've got a clean, airtight seal over the hole. If you're unsure which hole you are on, count three back from hole ten.

TIP 2
Blow gently while thinking "ah." Keep your tongue relaxed and the inside of your mouth open.

TIP 3
The tip of your tongue should be touching the inside of your bottom teeth. At the same time, the top two sides of your tongue should be touching the middle to back of your top teeth.

First-position blues scale

The blues scale for first position works nicely in the top octave of the harmonica. That's because our blow bends end up falling on juicy notes in that first-position scale. It's a bit challenging at first, but quite exciting once you've got it mastered. Practice this one in both directions

C	Eb	F	Gb	G	Bb	C

(track # 7-44)

Following are some super sweet blow bend licks based on the first-position blues scale (played on a C harmonica). You can use these licks whenever you're jamming in first position and also over the IV (four) chord when you're in second position.

$$+9 \frown \ 9 \ 10 \frown \ \sharp 10 \ 9 \frown \ +9 \ 9 \ 8 \ 7$$

$$+8 \frown 8 \ 9 \ +9 \frown 9 \frown +9 \ 9 \ 8 \ 7$$

$$+9 \frown 9 \ 10 \quad +9 \frown 9 \ 10 \quad +9 \frown 9 \ 10 \quad 9 \frown +9 \ 8 \ 7$$

TIP 4

Purse your lips a bit tighter and scrunch your mouth closed, leaving only a pea-sized opening inside and at the very front of your mouth. As you do this try to aim your airstream in a downward direction and change from an "ah" sound to a "yoo" sound.

♪ CHAPTER 8 ♫
NUTS AND BOLTS

THIS SECTION:

🎼 CHAPTER 8: **NUTS AND BOLTS**

There is no shortage of ways to produce a myriad of impressive sounds and cool effects on the harmonica. The next four techniques—tremolo, vibrato, warbles, and tongue blocking—are some of the most commonly used and heard on the harmonica. Be patient with each one, they can take some time to master. Once you have mastered them you'll be pleasantly surprised by how many more dimensions they add to your playing.

HAND TREMOLO

Tremolo can be defined as a "periodic change of volume or amplitude." A simpler way of describing it for us harmonica players is "wah-wah." The harmonica is known the world over for its fabulous "wah-wah" sound. To hear it in your head, try to picture the guy stuck in his jail cell pouring out a mournful melody on the harmonica, or how about a cowboy sitting next to a fire on a chilly evening blowing on a verse or two of "Oh Shenandoah" with his rusty old harmonica? What do both of these images have in common? Tremolo (and a harmonica of course).

𝄞 CHAPTER 8: NUTS AND BOLTS

When tastefully applied, a bit of tremolo will make anything that already sounds good on the harmonica sound great, and the best thing is, it's easy to do. In fact, you might already be doing it without knowing it. Just in case you're not, here's the lowdown on producing a tremolo effect with your harmonica.

A tremolo effect on the harmonica happens when we mute the sound, un-mute the sound, mute the sound, un-mute the sound, mute the sound etc., always at a constant rate. The way we do that is by opening up our right hand to let the sound out and then closing it again to keep the sound in. This consistent fluctuation produces a tremolo effect. The speed at which you open and close your right hand will determine the speed of the tremolo. Where you open and close your hand and also to what degree that you open and close it will determine the depth of the tremolo. Here's what it sounds like: ***track # 8-1***.

Try this:

1 Hold the harmonica in both hands as described in Chapter 1.

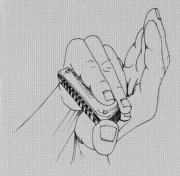

2 Gently blow out on hole two or three. Keeping the thumb in position, pivot your right hand open from the heels of your palms.

3 As you do this, keep the fingers of your right hand together so that they are touching one another. Pretend that they are super-glued together. In fact, if you are struggling to keep your fingers closed like that, then just go ahead and glue them together. STOP! Just kidding! Whew...

4 Now continue to open and close your right hand slowly, but at a consistent tempo. Can you hear a "wah" sound or something similar? Opening and closing your hand at different places will produce a different sounding tremolo.

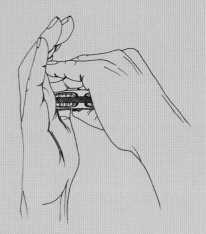

Try this one:

5 Open your right hand where the right side of it touches the left side of your left hand. Keep your right-hand thumb on the harmonica and use it as the pivot point. The great Sonny Terry used to take his right hand completely off the harmonica and fan it for a unique tremolo effect. There is no shortage of ways to experiment with tremolo.

♪ CHAPTER 8: NUTS AND BOLTS

"Oh Shenandoah"

Listen to "Oh Shenandoah" (***track # 8-2***), and then practice it slowly without adding any tremolo. After you become comfortable with the melody, add some tremolo to the last note of every phrase (grouping of notes). After you're comfortable with that, add the tremolo to whatever specific note(s) you think might sound good. Try the tremolo out at a few different tempos. There's no "wrong" way to do it, so experiment and have fun. After a while your own unique tremolo sound will emerge, and you'll be doing it without even thinking about it.

"There's no 'wrong' way to do it, so experiment and have fun. After a while your own unique tremolo sound will emerge, and you'll be doing it without even thinking about it."

#8-2 Oh Shenandoah

3 4 4 4   4 5 6 6 6   7 7 6   6 6 6 5 6

6 6 6   5 6 5 4 4   3 4   3 4 6 6

3 4 4 5   4 4 4

♪ CHAPTER 8: NUTS AND BOLTS

VIBRATO

While tremolo is defined as a periodic change in volume, vibrato can be defined as a periodic change in pitch or frequency. Unlike a bend, where the pitch changes by a semitone (to a new note) or more, vibrato usually changes the pitch by half a semitone or less. The main reason for using vibrato is to create greater expression and to add warmth to the music.

The terms vibrato and tremolo are often used interchangeably. In theory, it's difficult for anyone to achieve a pure vibrato or tremolo where only the pitch or only the volume is varied. Variations in both pitch and volume are often achieved at the same time.

For a harmonica player, vibrato can be described as a technique used to sound incredibly soulful while you're hanging out on a note. When you do this, your listeners can't help but respond with a "Yeah, man!" How's that for a clear definition?

However you want describe it, a good vibrato is HUGE when it comes to your tone and your tone is HUGE when it comes to sounding good.

There are numerous types of vibratos and numerous ways to produce them on the harmonica. We're going to learn the one most often found in the blues and referred to as throat vibrato. When producing a throat vibrato, your main goal is to open and close your vocal folds (vocal cords) at a constant rate, while either blowing out or drawing in. Sounds simple enough, but just wait...

"Hearing it helps it. Listen to a lot of harmonica players with good vibratos. Try to hear the same sound in your head each time you attempt to reproduce it."

Charlie Musselwhite onstage at the New Orleans Jazz & Heritage Festival 2011

♪ CHAPTER 8: NUTS AND BOLTS

Try this:

Listen to some throat vibratos on hole two, hole three, and then hole four, ***track # 8-3***.

Without the harmonica:

1 Blow out while making a whisper-like cough. Cough lightly but from deep in your throat. Now take a bit of the cough out of it but maintain the bursts of airflow being produced by the opening and closing of your throat.

With the harmonica:

2 Cover over hole two with your mouth and try it. Blow out and cough as above while keeping a steady stream of air flowing. Try to keep the pulsation at a steady rate.

Without the harmonica:

3 Do the same thing as above, but this time try it while drawing air in. Most people find drawing in and pulsating at a constant rate much more difficult than blowing out at a steady rate.

With the harmonica:

4 Draw in on hole two while doing the same soft cough as described above. Your vibrato might be sporadic at first. That's okay. You also might find that it pulsates at a fairly quick tempo. Focus on keeping it steady and slowing it down. Learn to control the rate of the fluctuations. A nice throat vibrato will often intentionally pulsate in sync with the music. There are two ways to accomplish this.

1 Pulsate the vibrato twice for every quarter note (beat or foot tap).

2 Pulsate the vibrato three times (triplet) for every quarter note (beat or foot tap). While this isn't necessary for a nice sounding vibrato, it can add a cool dimension to your tone. When you're eventually able to control the pulsations, then try it out.

Producing a killer throat vibrato takes time. Be patient. Once you're able to make one, it will keep improving for as long for as you continue playing.

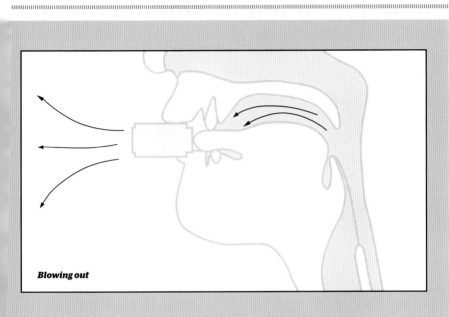

Blowing out

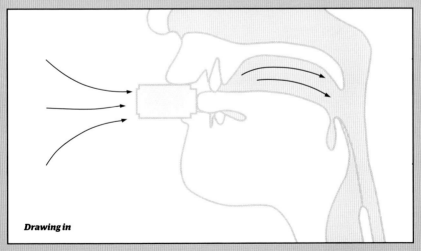

Drawing in

♪ CHAPTER 8: NUTS AND BOLTS

Sonny Terry and Brownie MaGhee

SHAKES, WARBLES, AND TRILLS (SUNG TO THE TUNE OF "SHAKE, RATTLE, AND ROLL")

At this point you might find yourself a bit worn out from one new technique after another. You might like to try something else for a while? Sorry, can't do that just now. But you'll find that this one is fast, easy, and fun, not to mention that it sounds good too.

The spectacular " shake" is also known as the fabulous "warble" and occasionally referred to as the legendary "trill." Trying to remember those three names is going to be the hardest thing about learning to play them. For the purposes of this book, we'll refer to this technique as the shake.

Playing between two adjacent holes on the harmonica, back and forth, produces a shake. You'll be shaking your head back and forth while keeping a continuous breath in or out. The note on the left will be the starting note and also the primary or melody note. As the alternating speed is increased, the note in the right hole intertwines audibly with the note on the left hole. In doing so, a new texture or sound is created.

It's likely that you've heard a shake before if you've ever listened to any blues harmonica. If you've ever seen a blues band and watched the harmonica player shaking his head back and forth repeatedly, as if he's got a hornets' nest stuck in his ear, then you've witnessed a shake. Now it's time to play one (***track # 8-4***).

♪ CHAPTER 8: NUTS AND BOLTS

Let's try it:

1 Place your lips squarely over hole four and breathe in.

2 Slowly begin to move your head back and forth (to the right first) between holes four and five. Use a very subtle head movement as if shaking your head to say "no."

3 The slower you move your head back and forth, the more distinct the two notes will be. The faster you go the more the two notes will begin to blur together.

Both notes should sound with equal volume, clarity, and constancy. If you start losing any of those, slow down until you've regained it. Gradually increase the speed each day making sure to maintain all of the above.

The shake can be done both by blowing and drawing. The most common hole combinations to play a shake on are three-four, four-five, and five-six. Shakes also sound good while simultaneously bending a note, but this is more challenging.

Moving your head back and forth can be a dizzying experience for some people. If that's the case for you, here's another way. Keep your head still and move the harmonica horizontally with your hands. Either method sounds good. Just make sure to maintain the evenness and clarity.

There you have it, the shake.

"Imagine that you're at a very noisy, crowded company picnic with your family. As you glance to your right, you notice your six-year-old daughter across the park playing with your shiny, brand-new nine-iron golf club. She looks up at you, excited to have finally caught your attention. While standing directly over a very large rock, you can see her form the words "watch this, Daddy." Looking quite adorable, she raises the club over her head in preparation for a mighty swing at the massive stone below her. Searching for a lightning-fast response, you frantically begin shaking your head "no" with small but quick movements, much like an impassioned plea. You get the idea. Shakes are very similar to this, but you can leave out the rapid heartbeat and uncontrollable perspiration."

𝄞 CHAPTER 8: NUTS AND BOLTS

TONGUE BLOCKING

Up until now we've been getting all of our single notes by using the lip-pursing method. Another way to get single notes is through a method called tongue blocking. Lip pursing is easier to learn than tongue blocking (although you might not think so at the time). Lip pursing also makes it easier to learn bending and over blowing. Tongue blocking however, has it's own unique advantages and sounds. It's a good idea to learn both methods. Tongue blocking enables you to produce a bigger sound (tone), accompany melodies with chords, play two notes an octave apart simultaneously, and lots, lots more. Tongue blocking is definitely challenging at first, and can leave you literally tongue-tied. As you begin to progress however, you'll see that it's well worth the effort.

Tongue blocking can be accomplished by placing your mouth completely over four holes and then blocking the three holes on the left by using the tip of your tongue. This will allow only the note farthest to the right to sound.

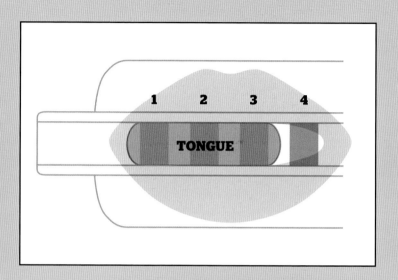

TIP *Covering four holes might feel like too much of a stretch at first. If that's the case, go ahead and cover just three holes with your lips (holes two, three, and four), blocking out holes two and three with your tongue. It will still sound good this way and you can try a bigger stretch later on as you get more comfortable.*

♪ CHAPTER 8: NUTS AND BOLTS

1 Start by opening your mouth wide and covering holes one, two, three, and four.

2 Gently blow so that holes one, two, three, and four are sounding together. Take long a breath as you do this.

3 Place the tip of your tongue on holes one, two, and three so that they are covered completely. At this point only hole four should be sounding.

4 Now try the same thing, but this time drawing in, again with long breaths. As with almost everything else on the harmonica, try to stay relaxed and make sure that your breathing and tongue are relaxed as well.

The following are five exercises that will help as you progress with your tongue blocking. Practice them in the order presented.

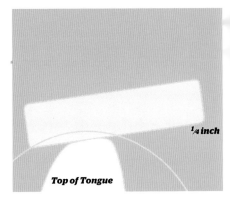

¼ inch

Top of Tongue

> *If you hear some leakage or still hear a note sounding from the left side, try this. Instead of placing the tip of your tongue on the harmonica, place the top of your tongue (about ¼ in/6 mm back from the tip) on the holes. You can also try bringing the very far right side of the harmonica slightly out (¼ in/6 mm or so), away from your face. When you do this the area of your tongue that is slightly left of the tip should be covering the holes. Experiment to find what works best for you. When you find it, use it.*

Exercise one

Remember the first-position major scale? We're going to be using it as we practice some different exercises using tongue blocks.

First-position major scale   4 4 5 5 6 6 7 7

Play up and down the entire scale while keeping your tongue blocked over two (or three) holes. The only note that should sound is the unblocked note on the right as you progress up and down the scale. Play it very slowly holding each note for four beats (foot taps). Try to play it cleanly so that only the notes in the scale are sounding.

....

Exercise two

Next, we're going to add in some chords along with our melody note. Cover holes one, two, three, and four with your mouth. Tongue-block the notes on the left leaving only hole four open. Blow a steady stream of air and hold it for four beats. Lift your tongue off and draw in for four beats so that a chord sounds. Keep doing this, back and forth, until you can hear a smooth transition. Now reverse the process. Start by tongue blocking the holes to the left, but this time draw in first, keeping your airstream steady, and hold it for four beats. Lift your tongue off and blow out for four beats. Alternate back and forth this way until it sounds smooth.

....

Exercise three

Now we are going to play up and down the scale switching our tongue on and off the harmonica. Hold each note for one full beat, but this time keep your tongue down over the holes on the downbeats (where your foot taps down) and then lift your tongue off on the up beats (where your foot comes back up). Try to "slap" your tongue down on the downbeats.

....

♪ CHAPTER 8: NUTS AND BOLTS

Tongue slap

As you slap your tongue back onto the harmonica, the air that was being used to sound the three or four holes while your tongue was up, is now redirected through the hole on the right. Think of "ha" as your tongue slaps down into position.

Exercise four

By now you should be feeling a bit more comfortable with tongue blocking, so let's try it out in a simple melody.

#8-8 Mary Had a Little Lamb

```
 ।    (  ।    ।                            ।  ।  ।
 5  ∧ 4  4  4 5  ∧ 5 ∧          5 ∧ 5 ∧         5 6 6 ∧
    (  (                        ।    ।

 ।    (  ।    ।                          ।     (     (
 5  ∧ 4  4  4 5  ∧ 5 ∧          4 ∧ 5 4  4 ∧ 4
    (  (                          (     (
```

Mary Had a Little Lamb

Your tongue should be continuously blocking the holes to the left unless you see the symbol ^, at which time you should move your tongue off the holes. Make sure to place your tongue back down before the next note sounds. Always keep a steady stream of air flowing until you have to change breath directions.

*There are myriad ways to tongue block this or any song. One variation would be to have the tongue move off the holes on specific melody notes instead of always between the melody notes. Listen to the following variation and then try to come up with one of your own (**track # 8-9**).*

THE TONGUE SPLIT

The tongue split allows you to simultaneously play a single note out of each side of your mouth. Wow, if you could only do that, juggle, and play a drum on your back at the same time, you'd have a long line of agents lined up at your door. Even without the juggling and the drum, it can take a bit of work to get it just right. Patience is the key (along with removing any gum from your mouth).

Tongue splitting allows you to play octaves together, which sound big and full. It also allows you to play certain harmony notes together, which would otherwise have been impossible.

Let's take a closer look. In this example, you will cover four holes with your mouth and place your tongue on the two holes in the middle. This is called the two-hole split. The choice of holes covered determines whether you are playing the octaves or the harmony notes. Some splits will produce neither and end up being dissonant.

Octaves

Hole-one blow and hole-four blow are both C notes but in different registers. To play these notes together, you would cover holes one, two, three, and four with your mouth. Then tongue-block holes two and three. It will sound like the two notes on each end (holes one and four) are blending into one big, full sounding note (**track # 8-10**).

Harmonies (notes that sound good when played together)

Hole-four draw (D) and hole-seven draw (B) harmonize with each other. To play this, you would need to cover holes four, five, six, and seven with your mouth and tongue-block the two middle holes (five and six) (**track # 8-11**).

♭ CHAPTER 8: NUTS AND BOLTS

Dissonance (notes that don't sound good when played together)

Hole-three draw (B) and hole-six draw (A) do not sound too good when played together. They are dissonant. You can use dissonance sounds to create a certain feel or mood. To play them, you would cover holes three, four, five, and six with your mouth. Then tongue-block the two middle holes (four and five). Listen on ***track # 8-12***.

Here are all of the two-hole splits that can be tongue blocked for octaves. Try them out.

Two-hole octave splits, blowing

Notes	C	E	G	C	E	G	C
Holes	1-4	2-5	3-6	4-7	5-8	6-9	7-10

Two-hole octave splits, drawing

Note	D
Hole	1-4

Here are the harmony splits.

Two-hole harmony splits, drawing

Notes	D-B	F-D	A-F
Holes	4-7	5-8	6-9

When you're more comfortable with the two-hole split, try using it in this next song. Each group of two notes is a two-hole split. Some of the splits will be octaves and some will be harmonies. The six-hole draw is always played by itself, as there are no octaves or harmonies that can be played simultaneously with it using a two-hole split.

#8-13 My Bonnie Lies Over the Ocean, using two-hole octave splits

```
 ( |    ( |    ( |         ( |          ( |
 36    58    58    47    58    47    6    6    36
              ( |          ( |              |    |
```

```
 ( |    ( |    ( |    ( |    ( |         ( |
 36    58    58    47    47    47    47    58
              ( |               ( |          ( |
```

```
 ( |    ( |    ( |         ( |          ( |
 36    58    58    47    58    47    6    6    36
              ( |          ( |              |    |
```

```
 ( |         ( |
 36    6    58    47    47    6    47    47
        |    ( |         ( |    |    ( |
```

The three-hole split is as the name implies. You will need to open your mouth even wider to cover five holes. Your tongue will then block out the middle three holes leaving the notes at each end to sound. As you attempt to cover five holes, place the harmonica deeper into your mouth to widen it. These are quite tricky.

Try out these three-hole splits.

Three-hole octave splits drawing

Notes	B	D	F	A
Holes	3-7	4-8	5-9	6-10

Tongue splitting the blues

Certain tongue-split combinations sound awesome with the blues; consequently, you hear a lot of blues harpists using them. The following is a slight variation on a standard blues lick. This will incorporate some tongue-blocked octaves and even some bluesy tongue-blocked dissonance. The back end of the lick has some "dirty" playing, as well as bending and lip smacking. Enjoy. (***Track # 8-14***).

#8-14

____Triplet____   ____Triplet____

I I   I I   I I   I I   I I   I I   I I
36   36   36   36   36   36   36

                    dirty

                    I I
25   I4   I4   34   2   I   2   I
I I   I I   I I   I   I   ≠   I

                    smack on hole 2

"These are just some of the many ways you can incorporate tongue blocking into your playing. There are lots more. Listen, experiment, and of course, have fun doing it."

MAINTENANCE AND REPAIR

Harmonica playing has evolved tremendously over its 150-plus years of existence. The last 20 or so years in particular have seen a remarkable paradigm shift in the creativity and skill-set of contemporary harmonica players. As such, this tiny piece of wood and metal is no longer considered a toy, but rather a versatile, expressive, and most importantly, a REAL instrument. As players have upped the ante with their skill levels, harmonica manufacturers have responded. Many new makes and models have emerged with increasingly improved consistency and quality—the one included in this pack is ideal for bgeinners. The price of an inexpensive ten-hole diatonic harmonica can start at $5 and easily go up to $300 or more for one of exceptional quality. In today's market, you can expect to find a good quality harmonica for $30 and upward. These are usually well-made, professional instruments. They will treat you well if you do the same with them. Following are a few basic dos and don'ts to help keep your harmonicas in good

"An inexpensive ten-hole diatonic harmonica can start at $5 and easily go up to $300 or more for one of exceptional quality. In today's market, you can expect to find a good quality harmonica for $30 and upward. These are usually well-made, professional instruments."

Do keep your harmonica in a case when you're not using it. Objects of all sizes and shapes can easily get stuck inside causing the note to buzz or to not sound at all.

Do rinse your mouth out after eating and before playing your harmonica. If you think dried saliva is hard to get unstuck, I won't even bother telling you about peanut butter and jelly... yuck.

Do keep your harmonica clean. Occasionally take a towel and wipe the cover plates and the holes. You can do this with hydrogen peroxide, isopropyl alcohol, or just plain water. If gunk builds up around the holes, take a toothpick, or something similar, and carefully scrape it off. Along with looking better, your harmonica will taste better too.

Don't play your harmonica too hard. This will eventually cause the metal reeds that vibrate inside to fatigue. When they do, the vibrations on that reed will slow down causing the note to go flat (out of tune). If you start to notice the same hole is consistently out of tune on your other harmonicas, work gently on your blowing/drawing technique. That will most likely be the cause.

Don't leave your harmonica out in extreme temperatures. That includes direct sunlight, the dashboard of your car, or stuffed into the mouth of your four-year-old's first snowman of the year. You get the idea...

Don't let anyone else play on your harmonica. Germs...'nuff said.

Troubleshooting

If a note doesn't sound right, or play right, or doesn't play at all, there could be any one of a number of things causing it. Here are some of the more common reasons, along with some simple solutions.

1 If a note that was sounding a few seconds ago suddenly stops sounding, there's a good chance that saliva is stuck inside. This will prevent the reed from vibrating. Cover your mouth over three to four holes while keeping the offending note somewhere in the middle of the pack. Blow and draw four to five times quickly but gently to loosen up the saliva. Then tap the harmonica (with the holes facing down) on your pant leg a few times to remove it. If it's still stuck, repeat the process.

2 If the harmonica has been sitting for a bit and a note won't sound when you first try it, dried saliva could be the culprit. With the cover plates off (see below) locate the reed that's not sounding. Take a toothpick and gently bend it up and away from the reed plate once or twice to unstick it from the reed plate. Be careful to not get the toothpick stuck between the reed and the reed plate.

Or

Remove the cover plates and look for any small object that might be stuck in the reed. This could be a very small thread, lint, or any number of things. Take a toothpick and very gently remove the object or bend the reed just enough to free the object.

3 If a blow reed is responding sluggishly, the gap (opening) between the blow reed and the reed plate might be too small. Remove the cover plates and look at the opening between the free end (tip) of the reed and the reed plate. There should be a very small amount of space between the two. If you can't see any opening or can barely see any opening, take a toothpick and gently open the gap by bending the tip of the reed up. It won't take much, but it might take a few tries until the reed settles back into place. With the cover plates off, test the reed to see if it's responding better. If not, repeat the process.

Open-harp surgery: removing cover plates and reassembly

Most harmonica cover plates are attached to the comb using two or four screws/bolts. To remove the cover plates from the comb, carefully unscrew the screws/bolts, putting them aside for later reassembly. Removing the cover plates will reveal two reed plates attached to a wooden, plastic, or aluminum comb. Ten reeds are riveted on to each of the reed plates. The blow reeds are riveted to the underside of the reed plate and the draw reeds are riveted to the outside of the reed plate.

When reassembling, the blow reed plate goes on top. Place the top cover plate (the one with the ten numbers on it) over the blow reed plate. The ten numbers should be on the front side of the cover plate where your lips will go. Place the bottom cover plate over the draw reed plate, which should be on the underside of the comb. Replace the screws on one side, screwing them in about three-quarters of the way. Replace the screws on the other side and also screw them in about three-quarters of the way. Make sure the cover plates are aligned correctly over the cover plates. Some harmonicas will snap in, letting you know that they are aligned properly. When you are satisfied that they are properly lined up, screw both sides the rest of the way down.

To learn more about customizing and tuning harmonicas, try looking online. There are some useful websites suggested on page 196

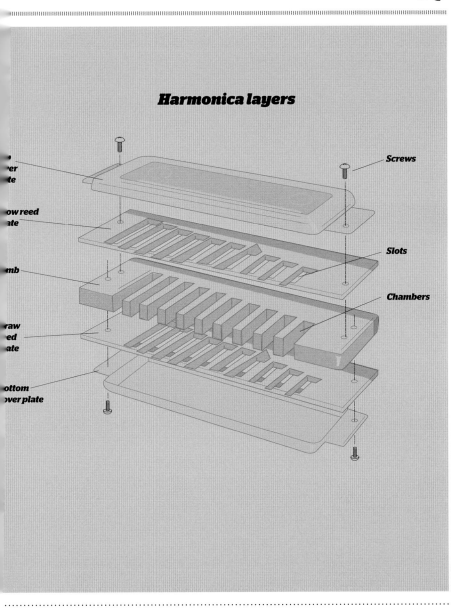

Harmonica layers

Screws

Slots

Chambers

...er ...te

...ow reed ...ate

...mb

...raw ...ed ...ate

...ottom ...over plate

𝄞 CHAPTER 8: NUTS AND BOLTS

O kay, so you've learned how to play, and you want to show off and join in a jam session... but there are a few simple rules of **harmonica etiquette** that you should be aware of. In fact, you might already be aware of some of them without even knowing it. Take this short multiple-choice quiz to find out how good your knowledge of jam-session etiquette is. Good luck.

1 You're in a nightclub watching a band or hanging out at a jam session. You'd really like to sit in and play. You should:
a) Have your friends shout out repeated and annoying requests for songs that you know how to play, until they let you join in.
b) Stay seated in the audience and play as loud as you can until they notice you.
c) Wait to be asked to join in with the music.

2 If you can't wait for them to ask you to join in, then:
a) Walk out angrily and teepee all of their houses.
b) Look menacingly at them while continuing to point to your watch.
c) Politely ask if you can join in.

3 You've been invited to sit in and jam, what's next?
a) Immediately let them know the song you'll be doing, the key, and where they should come in. Make it clear to them that they'll need to play with the proper dynamics during your solos.
b) Hand them a two-page introduction about yourself which you'd like them to recite when they bring you up on stage to play. Make sure that they practice it offstage first.
c) Wait your turn to play. Watch for cues from the bandleader or the session leader.

4 You're sitting in and you get the cue from the leader that it's your turn to play. You should:
a) Immediately ask everyone to stop playing because you're not sure of the position and key harmonica that you want to use. Take your time, figure it out, and then count the band back in four bars before your solo.
b) Go ahead and take your turn. If you've made any mistakes during your solo, then continue playing it over and over until you're satisfied with it. Soak in the glory.
c) Get in, say what you have to say (musically speaking) and then get out. Don't monopolize with long, extended solos. Less is more.

The answers.

You may be surprised to find out that for every question the correct answer is the letter "c." So how did you do on the test?
▶ If you scored four out of four, you're ready for prime-time jammin'.
▶ If you scored three out of four, you're almost there. Maybe take a veteran jammer with you the first few times.
▶ If you scored two or less, please don't let anyone know that you learned to play using this book.
Be honest about your musical abilities. If you end up in over your head nobody's going to have any fun. Use courtesy and good common sense and you won't go wrong.

♪ CHAPTER 8: NUTS AND BOLTS

HARMONICA MAKES AND MODELS

While the harmonica included with this book is great to learn and practice on at some point, your developing harmonica skills are going to require an instrument that suits you perfectly. While it's true that "the instrument does not make the player," a less-than-adequate instrument can be frustrating and make a good player bad. With that said, it can be well worth the price of investing a few extra dollars to have a better harmonica. It will not only play and sound better, but will be a lot more inspiring as well.

There are many harmonica manufacturers out there. Each one produces an assortment of ten-hole diatonic harmonicas. As you make your way on your harmonica journey, starting with the one included with this book, it's a good idea to try out different makes and models to find out which one(s) resonate best with you and your style. Since most harmonicas in the price range of $30 or higher are well-made instruments, choosing the right harmonica for you will mostly be a subjective thing. How do the cover plates feel on your mouth? Do the notes respond well to how soft or hard you play? Is the harmonica too bright or too dark for your taste etc.? As your playing evolves, the type of harmonica you require will evolve as well.

Buying harmonicas online usually means you will be offered a bit of a discount, especially when buying more than one at a time. Here are a few good online harmonica distributors. Each has a large assortment of brands, makes, and models for you to check out:

Sonny Boy
Williamson

𝄞 CHAPTER 8: NUTS AND BOLTS

CLUBS

There are more resources and networking opportunities than ever before to help you learn and grow your harmonica skills. Two well-known harmonica clubs are:

SPAH (The Society for the Preservation and Advancement of the Harmonica)

SPAH is based in the U.S.A. and Canada and hosts an annual convention along with a quarterly magazine. To find out more about SPAH and local harmonica clubs in your area, go to **www.spah.org**.

NHL (National Harmonica League)

The NHL is based in the United Kingdom. They publish a magazine entitled *Harmonica World*. To find out more, go to **harmonica.co.uk.**

WEBSITES

A great way to meet and learn from other harmonica players worldwide is through online discussion groups. Listed below are a few of the more prominent ones.

Harp-L
www.harp-l.com

HarpTalk
launch.groups.yahoo.com/group/harptalk

For an assortment of video harmonica lessons that can be downloaded and accessed directly on your computer, check out **www.sandyweltmanmusic.com** or **www.onlinelessonvideos.com** All of these lessons are 30-40 minutes in length and most come with play-along tracks and tablature.

There are tons of harmonica sites, many with good information and instruction. Google harmonica, blues harp, diatonic harmonica, or anything similar and watch a world of harmonica information open up at your fingertips.

Paul Butterfield

SUGGESTED LISTENING

Next to practicing, the best way to learn the harmonica is by listening to other great players. It's easy and fun to do. It also provides one of the most important things you'll need in order to keep improving, inspiration.

Below is a short list of some of the blues harmonica masters from years past. Each one has contributed to the harmonica in their own way. As you listen, see whose playing moves you the most, then keep on listening.

Sonny Terry: *The Folkway Years, 1944-1963* (Smithsonian Folkways)

Sonny Boy Williamson 1: *The Original Sonny Boy Williamson, vol 1* (JSP Records)

Sonny Boy Williamson 2 (Rice Miller): *His Best* (Chess Records)

Little Walter: *The Best Of* (Chess Records)

Paul Butterfield: *The Paul Butterfield Band, East West Live* (Winner Records)

Some of the more modern players worth checking out include: Howard Levy, John Popper, Carlos del Junco, Jason Ricci, Annie Raines, and many more.

TEN TIPS FOR BEGINNERS

1 Find a good instructor for private lessons or a lesson plan in a book or video etc. Hey... how about this book? Downloadable lessons are also available at www.sandyweltmanmusic.com (yet another shameless plug). You could also attend harmonica workshops and seminars.

2 Commit to learning harmonica for at least three months. Learning anything takes time and the harmonica requires some challenging (but exciting) techniques for beginners.

3 Listen often to other harmonica players (live or on recordings) that get you fired up and passionate about learning.

4 Play daily, even if it's only for five minutes. Five or ten minutes each day will take you farther in a shorter time than an hour once a week.

5 Make your practices intentional and structured. Make sure that your routine incorporates not only a time for fun but also a time for the challenges as well.

6 Find and use some of the many resources available today. There is so much amazing software that will support your practice. Much of it is fairly inexpensive or even available for free on the Internet.

7 Record yourself every so often. It's important to listen to your own playing and hear the progress you're making.

8 Be patient, especially if you've never learned an instrument before. Some of the more important techniques on a harmonica can be challenging at first. Understand that if you stick with it, you WILL be successful.

9 Learning anything new is bound to be frustrating from time to time. When that happens, put the harmonica down for a while and come back to it later. It's amazing how much progress can be made when you take a break from playing every now and then.

10 When you feel ready, get out there and jam along with others (see page 192). Playing along with a friend or two will build your confidence. As your confidence grows, so will your musicianship.

FINAL THOUGHTS

That's about it folks. I'm all out of words, wisdom, and wit (loosely defined). As this book comes to an end, your harmonica journey is just beginning.

You may have begun to notice that harmonica playing can be quite addictive. Life as you know it will never be the same again. That's why I've started H.P.A. (Harmonica Players Anonymous), a 12-step program dedicated to restoring life back to normal for harmonica players everywhere. Unfortunately, H.P.A. has so far been hugely unsuccessful. Harmonica playing continues to permeate the planet.

WARNING: From this point forward, you might find that most of your waking moments involve harmonica-related thoughts. You may start shutting out important people in your life in favor of playing the harmonica. If either of those things (or worse) starts to happen, please consider joining Harmonica Players Anonymous. Unfortunately I'm not at liberty to include any contact information for H.P.A. (after all, it is anonymous). However, take comfort in the fact that even as your life begins a downward spiral toward harmonica stuff 24/7, you're not alone. Thousands of kindred harmonica souls all over the world will be praying for you. So, keep the faith and remember that your sacrifice is not in vain. After all, a harmonica player is often greatly appreciated, and especially by his fellow inmates. Enjoy!

Sandy Weltman

Please check out my website where you can find additional information to enhance your harmonica playing, and get additional online learning instruction.
www.sandyweltmanmusic.com

♩ CHAPTER 9 ♫
MORE POPULAR MELODIES

The following songs can be played in the second and third octaves of the harmonica without the use of bent notes. Audio examples of each song (and more) can be heard by going to **www.sandyweltmanmusic.com** and clicking on the instruction books link. Enjoy.

Jesu, Joy Of Man's Desiring

5 4 4 5 6 5 5 6 6 6 7 7 7 6 5 4 4 5 5 6 6 6 5 5

4 5 4 3 4 4 2 3 4 5 5 4

5 4 4 5 6 5 5 6 6 6 7 7 7 6 5 4 4 5 4 6 5 5 4 4

2 4 3 4 5 6 7 6 5 4

Aura Lee (Love Me Tender)

6 7 7 7 8 6 8   7 7 6 7 7

6 7 7 7 8 6 8   7 7 6 7 7

8 8 8   8 8 8   8 8 7 8 8   8 8 9 8 8 6 8   7 7 6 7 7

Swannee River

5 4 4 5 4 4 7 6 7   6 5 4 4

5 4 4 5 4 4 7 6 7   6 5 4 4 4 4

7 7 8 6 6 6 6   7 7 6 5 6 6

5 4 4 5 4 4 7 6 7   6 5 4 4 4 4

Wayfarin' Stranger

4 4 6 6   6 6 6 5 4   4 4 6 6   4 5 6 6

4 4 6 6   6 6 6 5 4   4 4 6 6   6 6 5 4 4

6 6 7 8   7 8 7 6 7   6 6 7 8   7 6 6 6

4 4 6 6   6 6 6 5 4   4 4 6 6   6 6 5 4 4

Dixie

A)

6 5 4 4 4 4 5 5 6 6 6 5   6 6 6 6 6 6 6 7 7 8 8

7 6 7   6 5 6   4 5 4

B)

6 7 8 8 7 6 7 7   6 8   6 8   6 7 8 8 7 6 7 7 6 6 5

7 5 5 4   5 4   5 4   6 6 5 8 7 8 7

5 4   5 4   6 6 5 8 7 8 7

Maison Bourbon
DEDICATED TO THE
PRESERVATION OF JAZZ
Heineken

The Arkansas Traveler

A)

7 8 8 7 6 6 6 6 7 8 8 8 8 8 8 8 7 6 6

7 8 8 7 6 6 6 6 7 7 7 7 6 6 7 6 5 5 4 4 3 4

B)

9 9 8 9 9 8 8 9 8 8 7 8 8 7 7

7 7 7 8 8 8 7 8 8 7 7 6 6

9 9 8 9 9 8 8 9 8 8 7 8 8 7 7

7 7 7 6 6 7 6 5 5 4 4 3 4

Danny Boy

A)

7 7 8 8   8 8 10 9 8 8 7 6   7 8 9 9

10 9 8 7 8 8   7 7 8 8   8 8 10 9 8 8 7 6

7 7 8 8   9 8 8 7 7 7

B)

6 6 7 7   7 7 6 6 6 5 4   6 6 7 7   7 7 6 6 5 4

6 6 6 8   7 8 7 6 7 6 5 4   3 4 4 5 6 6 5 4 4 3 4 4

The Irish Washerwoman

5 4 4 3 4 4 5 4 5 6 5 5   5 5 5 4 6 5 5 4 4 4

7 7 7 6 5 6 7 7 7 8 8 7   7 6 7 6 4 6 7 6 7 8 7 7

6 7 7 6 7 7 5 7 7 5 5 6 5 5 5 4 6 5 5 4 4 4

Bonnie Banks Of Loch Lomond

7 7 8 8 8 8 7 7 6 6 6 7 7 8 9 10 9

10 10 9 8 8 9 9 8 8 7 6 6 7 8 9 10 9 8 8 7

𝄞 CHAPTER 9: MORE POPULAR MELODIES

Star of the County Down

A)

6 6 6 6 6 7 7 8   7 8 8 8 7 6 6 5 6

7 7 6 6 6 6 6 7 7 8   7 8 8 8 7 6 7 6 6

B)

9 8 8 8 7 7 7   7 8 8 8 7 6 6 5 6

7 7 6 6 6 6 6 7 7 8   7 8 8 8 7 6 7 6 6

Silent Night

6 6 6 5   6 6 6 5   8 8 7   7 7 6

6 7 7 7 6   6 6 6 5   6 7 7 7 6   6 6 6 5

8 8 9 8 7 7 8   7 6 5 6 5 4 4

𝄞 CHAPTER 9: MORE POPULAR MELODIES

God Rest Ye Merry Gentlemen

6 6 8 8 8 7 7 6 6 6 7 7 8 8

6 6 8 8 8 7 7 6 6 6 7 7 8 8

9 8 8 9 9 10 8 8 7 6 7 7 8   7 8 8 9 8 8 8 7 7 6

7 7 6 8 7 8 8 9 9 10 8 8 7 7 6

Deck The Halls

| | | | | | | | | | | | | | | | |
|6|5|5|4|4|4|5|4|4|5|5|4|5|4|4|3|4|

6 5 5 4 4 4 5 4 4 5 5 4 5 4 4 3 4

6 5 5 4 4 4 5 4 4 5 5 4 5 4 4 3 4

4 5 5 4 5 5 6 5 5 6 6 6 7 7 7 6 6

6 5 5 4 4 4 5 4   6 6 6 6 6 5 5 4 4

Amazing Grace (first position)

Amazing Grace (second position)

𝄞 INDEX

𝄞 INDEX

♪ CREDITS

The images in this book are used with the permission of the copyright holders stated below. (Images are listed by page number.) All other illustrations and pictures are © Quintet Publishing Limited. While every effort has been made to credit contributors, Quintet Publishing would like to apologize should there have been any omissions or errors and would be pleased to make the appropriate corrections for future editions of this book.

7 Shutterstock; 8 iStock; 15 iStock; 17 iStock; 25 Shutterstock; 26 Chev Wilkinson; 28 iStock; 35 iStock; 37 iStock; 38 Shutterstock; 39 Shutterstock; 41 Shutterstock; 42 iStock; 47 Corbis; 51 iStock; 53 Shutterstock; 59 iStock; 60 Shutterstock; 63 Lebrecht Music & Arts; 64 Shutterstock; 66 Shutterstock; 77 Corbis; 83 Lebrecht Music & Arts; 85 Corbis; 89 Corbis; 90 Shutterstock; 93 Shutterstock; 94 iStock; 95 Shutterstock; 101 Shutterstock; 111 iStock; 115 iStock; 118 Shutterstock; 120 iStock; 125 STARSTOCK; 127 iStock; 135 Shutterstock; 140 Shutterstock; 155 Jared Milgrim; 157 Getty Images; 158 Shutterstock; 162 iStock; 166 Shutterstock; 169 Corbis; 172 Corbis; 175 Shutterstock; 186 iStock; 187 Shutterstock; 192 2010 The Washington Post; 195 Lebrecht Music & Arts; 196 Photo courtesy of Hohner, Inc. USA; 197 Lebrecht Music & Arts; 198 iStock; 203 iStock; 206 Shutterstock; 209 Alamy; 212 Shutterstock; 213 Shutterstock; 219 Shutterstock

Many Special Thanks:

To my wife Jeanne, thanks for your timeless love, support, and much appreciated help... and lest I forget, your illustrations are an awesome addition as well. Also to my daughter Grace, you inspire me just by being your adorable self. I love you both more than all of the harmonicas in the world times infinity.

To my editor Liz Jones, thanks for keeping things organized and moving forward. It's been a real pleasure working with you. I hope to actually meet you someday.
Lastly but most importantly, for the many gifts and blessings in my life, my eternal gratitude goes out to my Lord and Savior Jesus Christ.